Cooperative Extension

Home*A*Syst

An Environmental Risk-Assessment Guide for the Home

Written by

Elaine Andrews
Ray Bosmans
Richard Castelnuovo
Carl DuPoldt
Karen Filchak
Carolyn Johnson
Barbara Kneen Avery
Lori S. Marsh

Alyson McCann
Bill McGowan
Shirley Niemeyer
Kathleen Parrott
Dean Solomon
K. Marc Teffeau
Michael P. Vogel

Editor

David J. Eagan

Designer

Cathleen Walker

This Publication Developed by
the National Farm*A*Syst/Home*A*Syst Program in Cooperation with
the Natural Resource, Agriculture, and Engineering Service (NRAES)

Santa Clara Valley
Water District

**Compliments of the
Santa Clara Valley
Water District**

NRAES–87
April 1997

ISBN 0-935817-30-1

Natural Resource, Agriculture, and Engineering Service (NRAES)
Cooperative Extension, 152 Riley-Robb Hall
Ithaca, New York 14853-5701

Phone: (607) 255-7654
Fax: (607) 254-8770
E-mail: NRAES@CORNELL.EDU
Web site: WWW.NRAES.ORG

Authors

Elaine Andrews
Environmental Education Specialist
Environmental Resources Center
University of Wisconsin Cooperative Extension

Ray Bosmans
Regional Extension Specialist
Home and Garden Information Center
University of Maryland Cooperative Extension

Richard Castelnuovo
Staff Attorney
National Farm*A*Syst Office
Madison, Wisconsin

Carl DuPoldt
Environmental Engineer
Natural Resources Conservation Service

Karen Filchak
Extension Educator
University of Connecticut Cooperative Extension

Carolyn Johnson
Water Quality Education Specialist
University of Wisconsin Cooperative Extension

Barbara Kneen Avery
Extension Associate
College of Human Ecology
Cornell Cooperative Extension

Lori S. Marsh
Associate Professor and Extension Engineer
Department of Biological Systems Engineering
Virginia Polytechnic Institute and State University

Alyson McCann
Water Quality Program Coordinator
University of Rhode Island Cooperative Extension

Bill McGowan
Agriculture/Water Quality Extension Educator
University of Delaware Cooperative Extension

Shirley Niemeyer
Professor and Extension Specialist
Environment of the Home/Housing
University of Nebraska–Lincoln

Kathleen Parrott
Associate Professor and Extension Housing
Specialist
Virginia Polytechnic Institute and State University

Dean Solomon
District Extension Natural Resources Agent
W. K. Kellogg Biological Station
Michigan State University Extension

K. Marc Teffeau
Regional Extension Specialist
Wye Research and Education Center
University of Maryland Cooperative Extension

Michael P. Vogel
Professor and Extension Housing Specialist
Montana State University Extension Service

Table of Contents

Table of Contents

Table of Contents

INTRODUCTION

*by Barbara Kneen Avery, College of Human Ecology, Cornell Cooperative Extension
and David J. Eagan, Home*A*Syst Editor*

What Is *Home*A*Syst?*

Home*A*Syst is a confidential, self-assessment program you can use to evaluate your home and property for pollution and health risks. In every home—large or small, new or old, city or country—there are potential pollution sources that can affect the health of your family, your community, or the environment.

Your drinking water, for example, can be affected by many potential contaminant sources: poorly maintained septic or sewage systems, leaky fuel tanks, lead pipes, fertilizers, pesticides, and hazardous household products. Hazards such as lead-based paint exist in older homes, while in newer, tightly sealed homes, indoor air pollution is often a problem. These and other risks can be reduced or eliminated if proper steps are taken. Even simple changes in household practices can prevent pollution and help reduce consumption of water, energy, and other resources.

Who Should Use This Book?

This easy-to-use assessment program will be a valuable reference for residents of rural and suburban homes. It is for those who care about their health and the environment and who are willing to take steps—no matter how small—to improve how they manage their homes. Whether you rent a room or own a house, this book can show you how to reduce your impact on natural systems and cut back your use of the earth's resources. *Home*A*Syst* can also help you protect your investment by identifying pollution risks on your property *before* expensive problems occur.

What Is Inside?

The eleven chapters in *Home*A*Syst* cover essential topics that every resident or homeowner should understand. Each chapter contains key points, along with tables of assessment questions, to help you understand which risks may apply to your situation. For some topics, this guidebook offers all the information you need to minimize or eliminate a pollution risk. For others, it provides a starting point and helps you locate further information and assistance. Keep in mind that laws and regulations can vary by state, county, city, or town. Check with local officials to make sure that your home practices or changes you plan to make comply with the law.

Getting Started

You can do *Home*A*Syst*'s assessment exercises one at a time or all together — it's up to you. The main idea is to take the time to identify any risks to your family's health or pollution threats to your local environment; then, where feasible, to take voluntary actions to reduce those risks and prevent problems.

This guidebook helps you accomplish three important objectives:

✔ Objective 1: Identify environmental risks, concerns, or problems in and around your home.

✔ Objective 2: Learn about better home and property management and find further information.

✔ Objective 3: Take preventive actions to safeguard your health and the environment.

These objectives are further explained below and illustrated using excerpts from chapter 6, "Lead In and Around the Home: Identifying and Managing Its Sources." This will help you become familiar with how *Home*A*Syst* works before starting the assessments.

Objective 1: Identify environmental risks.

Do you have pollution or health risks at home? Each *Home*A*Syst* chapter explains what risks to look for and why you should be concerned about certain conditions around your home. Here is an example from chapter 6 on sources of lead:

➤ *Does your interior paint contain lead, and what is its condition?*

Lead-based paint (LBP) is the most common source of high lead exposure for children. Most exposure, however, comes from contact with contaminated household dust rather than from eating paint chips. As paint ages or as painted surfaces rub against each other, lead-containing dust is created. If your LBP is perfectly intact, then the potential risk of accidental ingestion is greatly reduced. But if lead paint is cracking, chipping, flaking, or being rubbed by contact, then the danger of lead exposure is much higher.

In each chapter, assessment tables like the sample one below help you determine your potential level of risk.

Objective 2: Learn about managing your home and property.

Each chapter describes safe practices and gives recommendations for reducing or eliminating risks. To help you find further information on a topic, each chapter also recommends books, publications, telephone hotlines, and other resources. Here is what chapter 6 says about dealing with lead-based paint:

➤ *If you find lead…*

Remodeling or renovating in areas having LBP is especially risky. Scraping, sanding, or burning LBP creates extremely hazardous conditions, and strict precautions need to be taken—especially if children, pregnant women, or pets are present. If possible, homeowners should use the services of a certified lead inspector and lead-abatement contractor. Paint removal, replacement of lead-painted parts (such as windows, door jambs, and moldings), liquid encapsulants (special paint-like products that cover a surface), and removal off-site of leaded surfaces are some of the options for dealing with lead paint. LBP removal by untrained workers who do not use the proper methods and equipment can create a much greater health hazard than just leaving the paint alone.

Objective 3: Take preventive actions.

With *Home*A*Syst*, nobody is looking over your shoulder to make sure you take preventive or corrective action. It is always your choice. At the end of each chapter is an action checklist where you can write the risks you identified and the actions you plan to take. If you have lead-based paint in your residence, yours might look like the checklist on the following page.

Why Is It Important to Take Action?

Simply identifying risks will not prevent problems. Consider the following reasons for making voluntary improvements, particularly for responding to medium and high risks identified at your home.

SAMPLE ASSESSMENT TABLE (from chapter 6, "Lead In and Around the Home")

For each question in the table below, indicate your risk level in the right-hand column. Although some choices may not correspond exactly to your situation, choose the response that best fits.

	LOW RISK	MEDIUM RISK	HIGH RISK	YOUR RISK
Lead-based paint (LBP) on exterior of house	No LBP, or LBP is present but intact. There is a lawn or dense landscape plantings around the side of the home.	LBP is weathered or chalking. There is LBP in the soil around the home, but foot traffic is kept away.	LBP is chipping, peeling, or chalking. There is bare soil or foot traffic below painted walls.	❏ Low ❏ Medium ❏ High
Major roadways	No major roadway nearby.		Major roadway within 85 feet.	❏ Low ❏ High
Lead-related industry	No lead-related industry or incinerators in the area.		Lead smelter, battery manufacturer or recycler, or other lead-related industry nearby.	❏ Low ❏ High

SAMPLE ACTION CHECKLIST (from chapter 6, "Lead In and Around the Home")

Write all high and medium risks below.	What can you do to reduce the risk?	Set a target date for action.
Interior paint has moderate levels of lead. Plan to remodel bedroom this spring.	*Contact licensed lead-abatement contractor about project assessment and cost. Contact local or state health department for recommendations and information.*	*One month from today: April 22*
High level of lead in tap water.	*Get information and install treatment system to remove lead.*	*One week from today: March 29*

To safeguard your health

If you are like most people, you spend a great deal of time in your home. If there are dangers in the air you breathe, in the water you drink, or from hazardous chemicals in your home, they need to be eliminated quickly and effectively. Unfortunately, many people don't know about their potential risks until it is too late and problems have occurred.

To prevent contamination of our water supply and other natural resources

Protecting groundwater and surface water quality is essential to you, your neighbors, and others "downstream." This is important whether your drinking water comes from a private well or from a municipal system. Because everything is connected, what you do and what others do will affect someone else. If we are not good stewards of our water, land, and natural resources, who will be?

To protect your financial investment

Your home is often your most valuable investment. Most states have property disclosure laws that require environmental assessments before owners can sell or transfer their property. Knowing about risks or problems today may help prevent costly cleanups, repairs, and legal troubles in the future. And it pays not only to take care of your own property but also to make sure others around you are using good management practices. Property values and tax burdens can be affected by pollution problems on your property as well as in your neighborhood or city. In addition, taking steps to cut your use of energy, water, or other resources can save you money in the long run.

Now It's Up to You.

These *Home*A*Syst* chapters are not difficult to complete, and doing them can result in important benefits. For example, if you have children at home, working together on the assessments can be a worthwhile educational experience for everyone. And actions you take to eliminate risks may improve your property's resale value. If you value a clean environment and healthy surroundings, then using *Home*A*Syst*—and making changes—will be a real investment in your family's and your community's future.

Checklist for Pollution Risks
In and Around the Home

Purpose

This checklist is a way to quickly scan for potential problem areas in your home. It will help you identify possible risks and introduce you to many of the topics discussed in this book. The chapters cover many other assessment questions about situations and practices not included in the checklist. If you identify potential concerns using this checklist, or even *think* there may be risks or areas needing improvement, please turn to the chapter on the appropriate topic.

Instructions

Using a pencil, answer the questions *yes* or *no*. If you don't know the answer, try to find out by looking inside at the corresponding *Home*A*Syst* chapter. You may need to locate your home maintenance records, ask family members or neighbors, or seek assistance and further information. The answers you give on this checklist — and on the assessment tables inside — are *confidential*. They are for your eyes only and are meant to help you take action.

CHAPTER 1 Site Assessment: Protecting Water Quality Around Your Home (see page 7)	YES	NO
Is your soil sandy or gravelly, allowing water to drain through it quickly?		
Is there a potential source of contamination —such as manure, pesticide, or fertilizer storage; a fuel tank; a septic system drain field; or eroding soil —on your property within 100 feet of a well, stream, lake, or wetland?		
Is the water table less than 10 feet below the soil surface?		
CHAPTER 2 Stormwater Management (see page 15)	YES	NO
Do the downspouts from your roof gutters empty out onto paved surfaces instead of onto grass, mulch, or gravel and thus keep rain from soaking into the ground?		
Are fertilizers, pesticides, or salts stored where floodwaters might reach them?		
Are some parts of your property, particularly slopes, sparsely planted and without mulch, exposing the soil to erosion?		
CHAPTER 3 Drinking Water Well Management (see page 23)	YES	NO
Has it been more than two years since your water was tested for bacteria and nitrates?		
Do you have a dug or driven well instead of a drilled well?		
Does your well casing extend less than 12 inches above the ground, or is there a low area where rainwater runoff can collect around the well casing?		
Do you have abandoned wells on your property that have not been properly filled and capped?		

CHAPTER 4 **Household Wastewater: Septic Systems and Other Treatment Methods** (see page 33)	YES	NO
Has it been more than three years since your septic tank was pumped or inspected?		
Have you noticed any signs of a failing septic system such as slow drains, odors, or soggy ground over the drain field?		
Do you have standard toilets and faucets instead of water-conserving fixtures?		
CHAPTER 5 **Managing Hazardous Household Products** (see page 47)	YES	NO
Do you use products without knowing whether or not they are hazardous?		
Do you ever pour hazardous substances such as antifreeze, oil, paints, stains, polishes, or solvents down a sink drain, down a storm drain, in a ditch, or on the ground?		
Do you burn plastics, batteries, or chemicals that could contaminate air?		
CHAPTER 6 **Lead In and Around the Home: Identifying and Managing Its Sources** (see page 61)	YES	NO
Was your home built before 1978 (the year lead was banned from residential paint)?		
Do children under the age of six live in your home?		
Are painted surfaces inside or outside your home peeling, chipping, or chalking?		
Does drinking water flow through lead pipes or contact lead solder?		
CHAPTER 7 **Yard and Garden Care** (see page 69)	YES	NO
If you use fertilizer, has it been longer than three years since you had your lawn and garden soil tested for nutrients?		
Do you ever use pesticides without reading the label or following the recommended doses or application instructions?		
Do you have areas of bare soil on your property that are susceptible to erosion?		
CHAPTER 8 **Liquid Fuels: Safe Management of Gasoline, Heating Oil, Diesel, and Other Fuels** (see page 75)	YES	NO
Do you store fuel for your lawnmower or other gas-powered equipment in nonapproved containers such as glass jars, plastic jugs, or rusted cans?		
Do you store fuel or heating oil in an underground storage tank?		
If you have an aboveground fuel tank, does it lack protection against spills or leaks —for example, a catch basin or concrete spill pad?		

continued on next page ▶

CHAPTER 9 Indoor Air Quality: Reducing Health Risks and Improving the Air You Breathe (see page 85)	YES	NO
Do odors, such as those from cooking, linger in the air in your home?		
In winter, do you often notice water condensing on the inside of windows?		
Have you noticed symptoms, such as irritated eyes, coughing, or sneezing, that most often develop when you stay indoors at home?		
CHAPTER 10 **Heating and Cooling Systems: Saving Energy and Keeping Safe** (see page 96)	YES	NO
Has it been more than two years since your fuel-burning heating system was inspected for proper ventilation and energy efficiency?		
Are your energy bills relatively large for the size of your home?		
Do you feel cold drafts around windows and doors in winter?		
Does your attic lack the recommended amount of insulation?		
CHAPTER 11 **Managing Household Waste: Preventing, Reusing, Recycling, and Composting** (see page 106)	YES	NO
Do you purchase products that you don't really need?		
Do you buy products wrapped in excess packaging?		
Do you throw away yard or food wastes that could be composted?		

Where do you go from here?

If you answered *yes* to any of the questions, there may be pollution risks or special health concerns you will want to investigate. Turn to the appropriate *Home*A*Syst* chapter to find out how to reduce these risks in and around your home. We recommend that you begin with chapter 1, "Site Assessment: Protecting Water Quality Around Your Home," because it gives basic information that will be useful as you work on other topics. Creating a site map, which is explained in chapter 1, can help you understand important relationships between your land, buildings, nearby water resources, and other features.

SITE ASSESSMENT:
Protecting Water Quality Around Your Home

by Alyson McCann, University of Rhode Island Cooperative Extension

Is your soil sandy or gravelly? Does it drain quickly? Does stormwater runoff from your property flow into a nearby lake or pond? Do you store hazardous chemicals on your homesite, and are they close to a well or next to a lake, stream, or river? This chapter will help you become familiar with your homesite and how you manage it so you can identify risks to water resources. Completing the chapter will provide background information you can use throughout this book. This chapter covers two areas:

1. *Physical Characteristics of Your Homesite.* Examples of characteristics include soil type and depth; depth to bedrock; depth to the water table; and location of wetlands, streams, or other surface water.

2. *Making a Map of Your Homesite.* A map of your homesite showing buildings, roads, and other constructed or natural features can help you identify potential sources of trouble.

Why should you examine your homesite's physical characteristics and how you manage your home?

What you do in and around your home can affect water quality — both below the ground and in nearby lakes, streams, wetlands, or coastal ponds. This chapter will help you identify some important characteristics of your homesite such as soil type, geology, depth to groundwater, and nearness to surface water.

It also invites you to draw a simple "aerial view" map of your homesite. Your completed map will show the locations of important features and help you identify activities in and around your home that may pose risks to your health and the environment. Remember—this assessment is a starting point. It is meant to encourage you to complete some, or all, of the other *Home*A*Syst* chapters. To begin thinking about how your activities and site conditions can harm water quality, see figure 1.1 below for some examples of bad practices.

❶ Washing spilled motor oil and grass clippings into storm drains
❷ Storing gasoline and other hazardous chemicals near children's toys
❸ Paving walkways instead of using porous material, thus increasing runoff
❹ Not separating garbage for recycling
❺ Improperly adjusting sprinklers — wasting water
❻ Planting flowers that may require fertilizers and pesticides around the well cap
❼ Burning garbage, which adds toxins to air that eventually settle on the ground

Figure 1.1 Examples of practices that may harm the environment or home residents.

What is a watershed?

The water from your tap and in nearby lakes or streams is part of a much larger water system. While not everyone lives next to a pond or stream, we all live in a *watershed* — the land area that contributes water to a specific surface water body, such as a pond, lake, wetland, river, estuary, or bay (figure 1.2). The landscape's hills and valleys define the watershed, or "catchment" area.

A watershed is like a bathtub. The watershed outlet — the mouth of a pond, lake, or river — is the tub's drain. The watershed boundary is the tub's rim. The watershed's drainage system consists of a network of rivers, streams, constructed channels and storm drains, wetlands, and the underlying groundwater.

Common activities — like driving your car or fertilizing your lawn and garden — can affect water quality, even when you do these things far from any shore. By paying careful attention to how you manage activities in and around your home, you can protect your watershed and the water you drink.

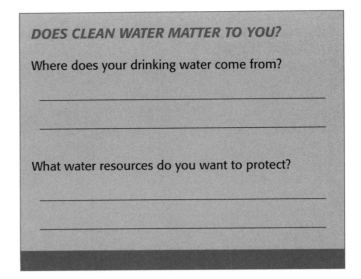

DOES CLEAN WATER MATTER TO YOU?

Where does your drinking water come from?

_____

_____

What water resources do you want to protect?

_____

_____

_____

What influences the quality of my water?

Understanding the site characteristics of your residence and the location of potential contamination sources are important first steps in safeguarding your water. In the hydrologic cycle, water moves through the air, over land, and through the soil (figure 1.3).

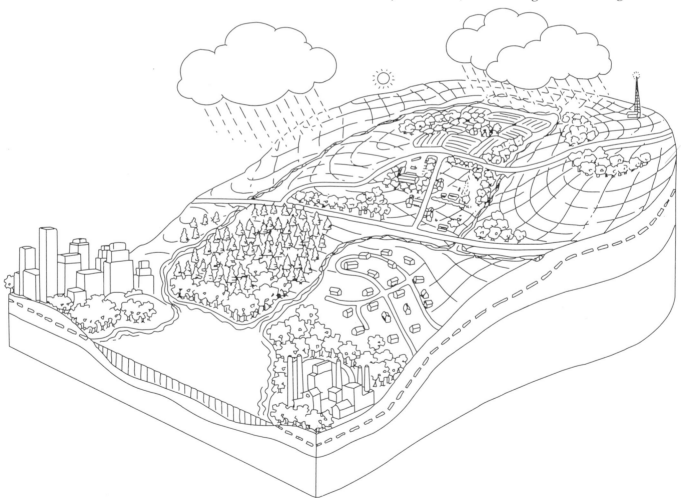

Figure 1.2 A watershed. Activities in the watershed can affect groundwater, stream, and lake quality at lower elevations in the watershed.

Physical characteristics, like soil type, depth to groundwater, and distance to surface water, may hasten or limit a contaminant's effect on water quality.

Water quality is also affected by many activities such as drinking-water well construction and maintenance, pesticide and fertilizer use and storage, septic system maintenance, waste disposal methods, and soil erosion. Animal wastes are another threat to water quality, particularly if large amounts from horses, dogs, or other animals are allowed to accumulate on your property. To protect your water, all of these factors need to be considered.

PART 1 — Physical Characteristics of Your Homesite

Every home comes with its own unique set of physical site conditions. You cannot change these conditions, but once you are aware of them, you can better understand risks that may result from activities you *can* change. At the end of part 1 is an assessment table to help you determine your potential risks. The information below will help you answer the questions in the table.

How can soil type affect water quality?

Soil plays an important role in determining where contaminants go and how water moves. Nearly all soils are permeable — which means water and other fluids can percolate, or seep, through them. Different soils have different properties that permit water (and contaminants) to percolate through the soil or run off at variable rates.

Chemicals applied to a lawn and wastes from a leaking septic tank, for example, can flow downward into groundwater or across the land into surface water. Many household activities can also produce problems that go beyond property boundaries. For example, contaminants that enter groundwater through a neighbor's abandoned well may flow underground until they reach *your* well.

What is your soil type?

Soil is grouped into three basic types based on particle size: clay, which has small particles; silt/loam, which has medium particles; and sand/gravel, which has large particles. You can get a good idea about your soil type by rubbing a moistened sample between two fingers. Is it sticky like clay, gritty and crumbly like sand, or somewhere in between like loam? Soil tests, which are offered through many Cooperative Extension offices, will also provide information on soil type.

How does soil type affect groundwater?

Groundwater is the water below the surface of the earth that, from the water table down, saturates the spaces between soil particles or fills cracks in underlying bedrock. Soil particle size influences which pollutants are able to reach groundwater. Some soils are better at trapping pollutants than others. Clay soils, which are made of tiny particles, slow the downward movement of water and in some cases can impede water movement completely. Sandy soils allow for rapid water movement, and silty soils occupy the middle range. Soils made of large particles pose the greatest risk, because water seeps downward through

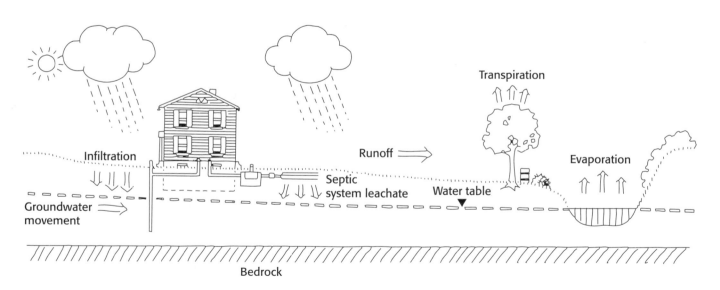

Figure 1.3 In the hydrologic cycle, water falls to the earth as rainfall and snow and returns to the atmosphere through transpiration and evaporation.

them readily without filtering out or decomposing pollutants. The ideal soil is a mix of midsize particles to allow infiltration and tiny particles, like clay or organic matter, to slow water movement and filter pollutants.

What are the risks to surface water?

Soil type can also affect surface water contamination. Although runoff occurs from all soil types, clay soils—which are least permeable—are more likely to cause surface water runoff. During a storm or flood, or even when watering your lawn, this runoff can wash contaminants from the land's surface into nearby surface waters. Eroding soil is also considered a water pollutant. Bare soil, especially on sloping land, can runoff into streams, rivers, lakes, or estuaries.

What is your soil depth?

The depth of soil influences risks to groundwater. Usually, the greater your soil depth, the farther water must seep down before reaching groundwater. Deep soils offer a better chance of filtering or breaking down pollutants before they reach groundwater. Generally, soils that are less than three feet deep present the highest risks for groundwater contamination.

How far down to reach bedrock?

Bedrock depth varies; it can be at the land's surface, just below the surface, or hundreds of feet down. The type of bedrock influences pollution risks. Shale, granites, and other impermeable types of rock make an effective barrier that blocks the downward movement of water and contaminants. Other rocks such as limestone can be highly permeable, allowing water to move freely into groundwater. When bedrock is split, or fractured, water can move through it unpredictably, spreading pollutants rapidly over long distances.

How deep is the water table?

If you dig a hole, you will eventually reach soil saturated with water. This *water table* marks the boundary between the unsaturated soil (where pore spaces between soil or rock contain air, roots, soil organisms, and some water) and the saturated soil, or groundwater (where water fills all pore spaces). In a wetland, the water table is at or just below the surface.

Your local water table fluctuates throughout the year but is usually highest in the wet months of spring and in late fall. In general, the closer the water table is to the land's surface, the more the groundwater is susceptible to contamination. Usually, a water table that is less than ten feet from the surface presents a higher risk for groundwater contamination.

HOW CAN YOU FIND OUT WHAT IS GOING ON UNDERGROUND?

There are several ways to find out about soil depth, bedrock type, and other features below the ground. Check your well-drilling records (if you have them), ask a neighbor who has a well, call a local well-drilling company, talk to your county extension agent, or call the local government office that gives permits for drilling wells. The Natural Resources Conservation Service maintains county soil surveys. The U.S. Geological Survey maintains groundwater maps.

Groundwater and surface water are interconnected. Groundwater generally flows downhill, following the same path as surface water, and eventually discharges into rivers, lakes, springs, wetlands, bays, or estuaries. If you keep impurities out of surface water but do not protect groundwater—or vice versa—contaminated waters may occur where you least expect.

Assessment 1 – Physical characteristics of your homesite

The table on page 11 is similar to the assessment tables in other *Home*A*Syst* chapters. For each question, three choices are given that describe situations or activities that could lead to high, medium, and low risks to human or environmental health.

Do the best you can. For some questions, your well-drilling records or local well drillers may be able to help. Some choices may not be exactly like your situation, so choose the response that best fits. Mark your risk level (low, medium, or high) in the right-hand column. Refer to part 1 above if you need more information to complete the table. If no choice is applicable, leave that line blank.

Responding to risks

Do not depend solely on the physical characteristics of your soil, bedrock, or other site features to protect water quality. You must take informed steps to prevent pollution. Although you can't change your soil type or the depth to bedrock, you can account for these factors when choosing home management practices that are better for preventing environmental problems. Note especially the medium and high risks you identified. Keep them in mind as you complete your homesite map and work on other *Home*A*Syst* chapters.

► **ASSESSMENT 1 — Physical Characteristics of Your Homesite**

	LOW RISK	MEDIUM RISK	HIGH RISK	YOUR RISK
Soil type and risks to lakes, rivers, wetlands, or other surface water from runoff	Sand/gravel (large particles)	Silt/loam (mid-size particles)	Clay (very tiny particles)	❏ Low ❏ Medium ❏ High
Soil type and risks to groundwater from infiltration	Clay (very tiny particles)	Silt/loam (mid-size particles)	Sand/gravel (large particles)	❏ Low ❏ Medium ❏ High
Soil depth	Deep (over 12 feet)	Moderately deep (3–12 feet)	Shallow (less than 3 feet)	❏ Low ❏ Medium ❏ High
Bedrock	Solid, not permeable or fractured	Solid limestone or sandstone	Fractured bedrock —any kind	❏ Low ❏ Medium ❏ High
Depth to water table	Over 20 feet	10–20 feet	Less than 10 feet	❏ Low ❏ Medium ❏ High
Nearness to surface water	Over 100 feet	25–100 feet	Less than 25 feet	❏ Low ❏ Medium ❏ High

PART 2 — Making a Map of Your Homesite

Why make a map?

By drawing a map of your homesite, you will take another step toward more fully understanding your pollution risks. Although your property has physical features you cannot change, there are many things that you can do to minimize risks. Your map will identify areas where you can focus your efforts. It will also assist you in completing other *Home*A*Syst* chapters. And if you involve children as you make your map and conduct the assessment, you will help teach them the importance of having clean water.

The materials you need to make your map are readily available: a measuring tape, a clipboard, a pencil, and the grid provided on page 14. The map you create will be an aerial view—the way your property would look if you took a photo of it from the air. A sample map is provided in figure 1.4 on page 12.

Potential sources of contaminants

Several home management practices and home site characteristics could have major effects on water quality. As you survey your property to make your map, be especially watchful for the following:

- Improperly located or unmaintained septic system or cesspool
- Underground or aboveground storage tank containing fuel oil, gasoline, or other petroleum products
- Improperly constructed or abandoned well
- Stockpiled animal waste or animal pens, corrals, or kennels close to a well or surface water body
- Improper storage, use, or disposal of yard and garden chemicals and other hazardous products like paints and solvents
- Machine maintenance workshop near well
- Road deicing materials that flow toward a well or nearby surface water body

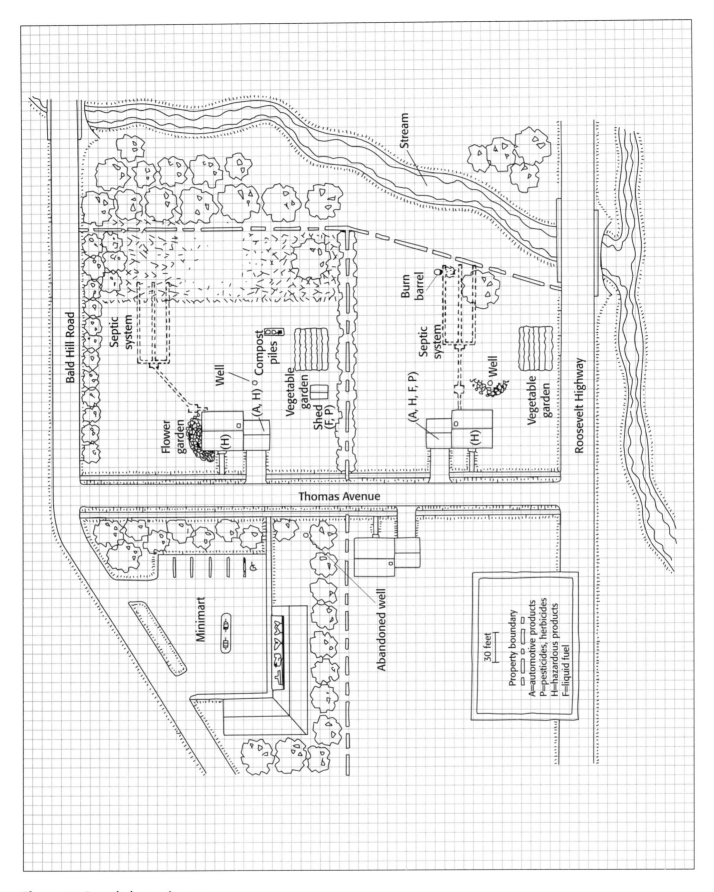

Figure 1.4 Sample homesite map.

       Home*A*Syst: An Environmental Risk-Assessment Guide for the Home

Instructions for your homesite map

Homesite features to include are:

- ☐ Property boundaries
- ☐ House and garage
- ☐ Outbuildings, sheds
- ☐ Septic system, drainfield
- ☐ Nearest surface water
- ☐ Water wells
- ☐ Dry or abandoned wells
- ☐ Heating oil or other fuel storage tanks
- ☐ Building perimeter drains
- ☐ Lawn areas
- ☐ Vegetable and flower gardens
- ☐ Other cultivated areas
- ☐ Animal waste storage areas
- ☐ Roads, driveways
- ☐ Drainage ditches
- ☐ Impervious surfaces (such as patios or sidewalks)

Location codes

On your map, note the areas where you store and use chemicals and other potential hazards by using letter codes. Make up your own code letters or symbols as needed. Examples are:

F = Fuel tanks for gasoline or heating oil

A = Automotive products like motor oil, gasoline, and antifreeze

P = Pesticides, herbicides

H = Hazardous products like solvents, acids, paints, and thinners

Other map-making ideas

For larger-view maps, add landscape features such as hills, rivers, and ponds and human-built features such as runoff drainways, roads, and bridges. Note potential sources of contamination beyond the boundaries of your property such as farm fields, dumps, and gas stations. Indicate seasonal changes at your homesite. For example, are there wet areas in the spring? Such areas might indicate a high water table.

Don't leave out things you cannot see

Inquire about previous or current industrial or agricultural activities in the area. Check with your town or city hall for information. Old landfills and buried fuel tanks are just a few examples of what you might find. Determine if any underground fuel tanks exist on neighboring properties. If there are tanks, septic systems, or other potential sources of contaminants upgradient (that is, *uphill*) from your well, they could affect the safety of your groundwater. These issues will be discussed in-depth in subsequent chapters.

Putting It All Together and Taking Action

The final step is to put both pieces of your assessment together — the assessment table results and map — so you can identify potential problem areas on your property. If you have rated any of the items in the table as medium or high risks and have identified potential contamination sources, then you should be concerned.

For example, you may have identified an underground heating oil tank or realized that you apply lawn or garden chemicals within 25 feet of a lake or stream. Perhaps your soil is sandy or your gasoline storage tank is close to your drinking water well. Is there an old abandoned well on your property that isn't properly sealed? To protect your family's health and the environment, and to safeguard your financial investment, you will want to take steps to correct these problems.

How Home*A*Syst *can help*

If you identify potentially hazardous or unsafe situations, what should you do? There are ten other chapters in this *Home*A*Syst* handbook that address specific concerns. For example, chapter 8 on liquid fuels contains information on the safe management of gasoline, heating oil, diesel, and other fuels. Chapter 3 will explain how to manage your private well water supply. These chapters and others will help you identify problems and develop an action plan for protecting your family's health and the local environment.

Home*A*Syst Helps Ensure Your Safety

This *Home*A*Syst* handbook covers a variety of topics to help homeowners examine and address their most important environmental concerns. See the complete list of chapters in the table of contents at the beginning of this handbook. For more information about topics covered in *Home*A*Syst*, or for information about laws and regulations specific to your area, contact your nearest Cooperative Extension office.

Contact the National Farm*A*Syst/Home*A*Syst Office at: B142 Steenbock Library, 550 Babcock Drive, Madison, WI 53706-1293; phone: (608) 262-0024; e-mail: <HOMEASYST@MACC.WISC.EDU>.

This chapter was written by Alyson McCann, Water Quality Program Coordinator, University of Rhode Island Cooperative Extension, Kingston, Rhode Island.

Graph Paper for Homesite Map

(one block = ¹⁄₁₀ inch = 10 feet)

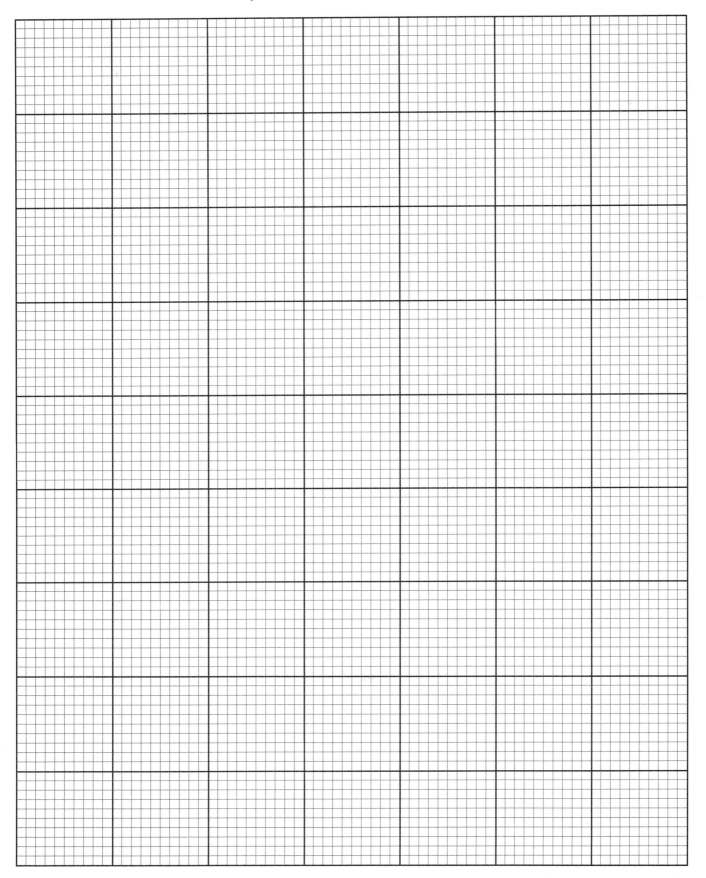

Chapter 2

STORMWATER MANAGEMENT

by Carl DuPoldt, Natural Resources Conservation Service and Carolyn Johnson, University of Wisconsin Cooperative Extension

This chapter examines potential risks to the environment and your health from stormwater runoff. Two areas are covered:

1. *Reducing Pollutants in Runoff.* Pollutants can include pesticides and chemicals, automotive wastes, grass clippings and yard waste, pet and animal wastes, and winter salt and deicers.

2. *Landscaping and Site Management to Control Runoff.* Some ways to help control runoff are preventing soil erosion, providing basement flood protection, landscaping, providing proper roof drainage, and minimizing paved surfaces.

Completing this chapter will help you evaluate how stormwater affects the environmental quality of your property and properties "downstream." You will also learn ways to reduce pollution risks.

What is stormwater, and why should you be concerned?

Stormwater is water from rain or melting snow that does not soak into the ground. It flows from rooftops, over paved areas and bare soil, and through sloped lawns. As it flows, this runoff collects and transports soil, pet waste, salt, pesticides, fertilizer, oil and grease, leaves, litter, and other potential pollutants. You don't need a heavy rainstorm to send pollutants rushing toward streams, wetlands, lakes, and oceans. A garden hose alone can supply enough water.

Even if your house is not on a waterfront, storm drains and sewers efficiently convey runoff from your neighborhood to the nearest body of water. Contrary to popular belief, storm sewers do not carry stormwater to wastewater treatment plants (figure 2.1).

| Storm sewer |
| - - - - |
| → Direction of storm sewer flow |

Figure 2.1 Runoff that flows into storm sewers goes directly to streams and lakes without treatment.

Polluted stormwater degrades our lakes, rivers, wet-lands, and ocean bays. Soil clouds water and degrades habitat for fish and water plants. Nutrients such as phosphorus promote the growth of algae, which crowds out other aquatic life. Toxic chemicals such as antifreeze and oil from leaking cars, carelessly applied pesticides, and zinc from galvanized metal gutters and downspouts threaten the health of fish and other aquatic life. Bacteria and parasites from pet waste can make nearby lakes and bays unsafe for wading and swimming after storms.

As many people have discovered, stormwater can be a problem closer to home. It can flow into basements and cause damage that is difficult and costly to clean up. Stormwater can also flow down a poorly sealed well shaft and contaminate drinking water. In areas with very porous soils or geology, pollutants in run-off may reach groundwater.

Across the country, public officials are turning their pollution control efforts from wastewater discharges to stormwater management in urban and rural areas. Stormwater pollution cannot be treated in the same way as water pollution from discharge pipes, because it comes from many sources (see table below). It is carried by stormwater from every street, parking lot, sidewalk, driveway, yard, and garden. The problem can only be solved with everyone's help.

COMMON SOURCES OF STORMWATER POLLUTANTS

Pollutant	Common sources
Silt, sand, and clay particles and other debris	Construction sites; bare spots in lawns and gardens; wastewater from washing cars and trucks on drive-ways or parking lots; unprotected streambanks
Nutrients	Overused or spilled fertilizers; pet waste; grass clippings and leaves left on streets and sidewalks; leaves burned in ditches
Disease organisms	Pet waste and garbage
Hydro-carbons	Car and truck exhaust; leaks and spills of oil and gas; burning leaves and garbage
Pesticides	Pesticides overapplied or applied before a rainstorm; spills and leaks
Metals	Cars and trucks (brake and tire wear, exhaust); galvanized metal gutters and downspouts

PART 1 — Reducing Pollutants in Runoff

Stormwater is unavoidable, but its effects can be re-duced by keeping harmful chemicals and materials out of the runoff. This section reviews potential sources of contamination and offers ways to minimize them. At the end of part 1, fill out the assessment table to help identify stormwater risks on your property.

Where does stormwater go?

The next time you are home during a rain shower, head outdoors with your boots and umbrella and watch where the rainwater goes. On a sketch of your property, draw arrows showing the direction that stormwater flows off driveways, rooftops, sidewalks, and yards. A sample map is provided in figure 2.2. (Instructions for making a homesite sketch can be found in chapter 1 beginning on page 11.) Does water soak into the ground quickly, or does it puddle in places and flow off lawns and driveways? Your soil type affects water infiltration (soaking into the ground). As you might expect, water infiltrates sandy soil quickly but has a hard time seeping into fine-grained silt or clay soils.

During your walk, note how far it is to the nearest storm sewer, ditch, wetland, stream, or body of open water. Note whether runoff flows onto your land from adjacent streets, lands, or stormwater systems. If you live at or near the bottom of a hill, you may have spe-cial problems. Be sure to go out during more than one rain shower to get a good understanding of runoff flow during small and large storms.

Are any car or truck wastes being carried away by stormwater?

Oil stains on your driveway and outdoor spills of anti-freeze, brake fluid, and other automotive fluids are easily carried away by a rainstorm. An oily sheen on runoff from your driveway is a sure sign that you need to be more careful. Pans, carpet scraps, and matting can catch drips. Routine maintenance can prevent your car from leaking and help identify potential leaks. If you change your own oil, be careful to avoid spills and collect waste oil for recycling. Oily car parts and fluid containers should be stored where rain and runoff can-not reach them. Never dump used oil, antifreeze, or gasoline down a storm drain, in a ditch, or on the ground. These wastes will end up in a nearby lake or stream, or they may pollute your drinking water.

Washing your car in the driveway creates runoff with-out the help of a rainstorm — your hose provides the water. The dirty, soapy runoff drains directly into storm sewers, picking up oil and other pollutants as

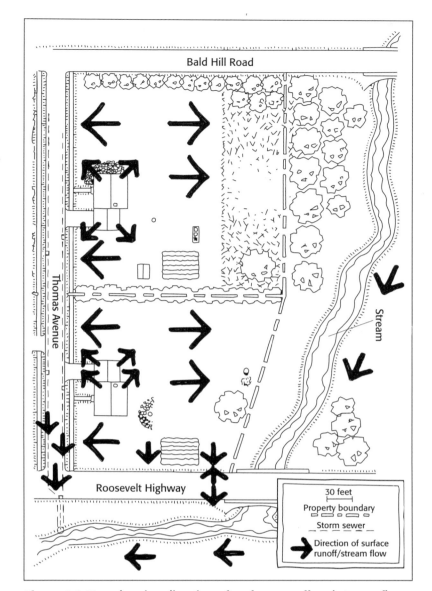

Figure 2.2 Map showing direction of surface runoff and stream flow.

it goes. Try washing your car on the lawn or, better yet, take it to a commercial car wash or spray booth that sends its dirty water to a wastewater treatment plant.

Are household products stored outside the reach of stormwater?

Most households store lawn and garden products like weed killers, insect killers, and fertilizers. If stormwater or floodwater reaches these products, it can transport them into surface water and possibly your well. Pool chemicals, salt for water softeners, and a wide variety of other chemical products can also cause trouble if they are washed away. Keeping such products in waterproof containers and storing them up high and out of the potential path of runoff or floods is important. You can avoid storage problems by buying only what you need for a particular task and then using up the product.

Do you use and handle chemicals safely?

Safe storage is only the first step in preventing contaminated runoff. When mixing chemicals, try to do it within a washtub so spills will be contained. If you spill chemicals, act quickly to contain and clean up the spill. This is particularly important on paved surfaces. Using more pesticides or fertilizers than you need invites problems. Timing of applications is also important. DO NOT apply pesticides and chemicals if rain is expected within twenty-four hours. See chapter 7, "Yard and Garden Care," for more information on the proper use and handling of yard and garden products.

Do you use road salt or other deicing product?

Road salt and deicers eventually wash off paved surfaces and end up in the soil or water. From your driveway or sidewalk, salt can readily flow to storm drains and into streams and lakes. Salt is harmful to wildlife and plants in high concentrations. Use less to keep these chemicals out of natural systems. If you use too much, clean up the excess. Consider sand or regular kitty litter as less toxic alternatives. Chipping ice off pavements is an even better choice, although care must be taken not to damage the pavement surface.

How are animal wastes kept from becoming a pollution problem?

Droppings from dogs and cats and from other commonly kept animals like exotic birds, rabbits, goats, and chickens can be troublesome in two ways. First, pet wastes contain nutrients that can promote the growth of algae if they enter streams and lakes. Second, animal droppings are a source of disease. The risk of stormwater contamination increases if pet wastes are allowed to accumulate in animal pen areas or left on sidewalks, streets, or driveways where runoff can carry them to storm sewers. Droppings that are not mixed with litter or other materials should be flushed down the toilet. Or, if local laws allow it, droppings may either be buried or wrapped and put in the garbage for disposal.

Are yard and garden wastes kept out of stormwater?

If left on sidewalks, driveways, or roads, grass clippings and other yard wastes will wash away with the next storm (figure 2.1, page 15). Although leaves and other plant debris accumulate naturally in streams and lakes, homeowners can contribute excess amounts of plant matter, especially in areas with many homes. This can lead to water that is unattractive or green with algae and unsuitable for recreation.

Burning yard waste is not an environmentally friendly alternative — and in some areas, it's illegal. Hydrocarbons and nutrients released by burning leaves contribute to water pollution as well as air pollution. Rain washes smoke particles out of the air, and runoff picks up dust and ashes left on pavement or in ditches. Avoiding the problem is easy — sweep clippings back onto the grass, and compost leaves and garden wastes on your property to recycle nutrients (figure 2.3).

Assessment 1 — Reducing pollutants in runoff
Use the table on the following page to rate your stormwater pollution risks. For each question, indicate your risk level in the right-hand column. Some choices may not correspond exactly to your situation. Choose the response that best fits. Refer to the sections above if you need more information.

Responding to risks
Your goal is to lower your risks. Turn to the action checklist on page 22 to record medium- and high-risk practices. Use the recommendations in part 1 to help you make plans to reduce your risks.

Figure 2.3 Sweeping grass clippings onto the lawn and composting help to keep yard waste out of storm sewers.

PART 2 — Landscaping and Site Management to Control Runoff
Some stormwater risks can be controlled by making changes to buildings, paved surfaces, the landscape, and soil surfaces. This section reviews some easily addressed problems, as well as major landscape alterations you might want to consider.

Are there areas of bare soil around your home?
Areas of bare soil often exist in vegetable and flower gardens, on newly seeded lawns, and around construction projects. Even on gentle slopes, water from rain and snow can remove large amounts of soil and carry it to wetlands, rivers, and lakes. Planting grass or other ground covers is the best way to stop erosion. Putting a straw or chip mulch over gardens or newly seeded areas will slow erosion. Straw bales, diversion ditches, and commercially available silt fences around construction sites can help slow runoff and trap sediment on-site. If you are working with a contractor, insist that precautions are taken to control runoff and erosion during construction.

Can you eliminate paved surfaces or install alternatives?
Concrete and asphalt roads, driveways, and walkways prevent rainwater from soaking into the ground. When you have the choice, consider alternative materials such as gravel or wood chips for walkways. Avoid paving areas such as patios. Where you need a more solid surface, consider using a "porous pavement" made from interlocking cement blocks or rubber mats that allow spaces for rainwater to seep into the ground. If you must pour concrete, keep the paved area as short and narrow as possible.

Is your basement protected from stormwater seepage or flooding?
Stormwater in your basement can be a hazard in two ways: first, if water carries contaminants or disease organisms into your home, and second, if water picks up chemicals stored in your basement and carries them into the sewer or ground. Basement windows or doors are common stormwater entry points and should be sealed against leaks. It is best if window and door sills are at least a foot above ground level. If windows are at or below ground level, they can be protected with clear plastic covers available in building supply stores. Window wells that extend above ground level can help divert stormwater. Your yard should be sloped away from the foundation to prevent water from pooling near the house and leaking into the basement.

► **ASSESSMENT 1 — Reducing Pollutants in Runoff**

	LOW RISK	MEDIUM RISK	HIGH RISK	YOUR RISK
Automotive wastes	Oil drips and fluid spills are cleaned up. Dirty car parts and other vehicle wastes are kept out of reach of stormwater runoff.	Drips and spills are not cleaned up. Car parts and other vehicle wastes are left on unpaved areas outside.	Used oil, antifreeze, and other wastes are dumped down the storm sewer, in a ditch, or on the ground.	❏ Low ❏ Medium ❏ High
Car washing	Cars and trucks are taken to a commercial car wash or spray booth.	Cars, trucks, or other items are washed on a lawn or gravel drive.	Cars, trucks, or other items are washed on a driveway, street, or other paved area.	❏ Low ❏ Medium ❏ High
Storage of pesticides, fertilizers, and other potentially harmful chemicals	Chemicals are stored in waterproof containers in a garage, shed, or basement that is protected from stormwater.	Chemicals are stored in waterproof containers but within reach of stormwater.	Chemicals are stored in non-waterproof containers outdoors or within reach of stormwater.	❏ Low ❏ Medium ❏ High
Handling and use of pesticides, fertilizers, and outdoor chemicals	Spills are cleaned up immediately, particularly on paved surfaces. Minimum amounts of chemicals are applied according to label instructions. Applications are delayed to avoid rain.	Applications are not delayed to avoid rain.	Spills are not cleaned up. Products are used in higher amounts than what is recommended on the label.	❏ Low ❏ Medium ❏ High
Pet and animal wastes	Animal and pet wastes are flushed down the toilet; buried away from gardens, wells, ditches, or areas where children play; or wrapped and placed in the garbage for disposal.*	Animal wastes are left to decompose on grass or soil. Wastes are scattered over a wide area.	Animal wastes are left on paved surfaces, concentrated in pen or yard areas, or dumped down a storm drain or in a ditch.	❏ Low ❏ Medium ❏ High
Grass clippings, leaves, and other yard waste	Grass clippings, leaves, and other yard wastes are swept off paved surfaces and onto lawns away from water flow routes. Leaves and other yard wastes are composted.	Leaves and other yard wastes are piled on the lawn next to the street for collection.	Grass clippings, leaves, and other yard wastes are left on driveways, streets, and other paved areas to be carried off by stormwater. Yard waste is burned on-site.	❏ Low ❏ Medium ❏ High

* Be sure to check local regulations regarding burying or landfilling pet and animal wastes.

Does roof water flow onto pavement or grass?

Your house roof, like pavement, sheds water. If downspouts from roof gutters empty onto grassy areas, the water will have a chance to soak into the ground. Aim downspouts away from foundations and paved surfaces (figure 2.4 on the following page). For roofs without gutters, plant grass, spread mulch, or use gravel under the drip line to prevent soil erosion and increase the ground's capacity to absorb water. Consider using cisterns or rain barrels to catch rainwater for watering lawns and gardens in dry weather.

Figure 2.4 Roof drainage should be directed to the lawn or a flower bed and away from the foundation and paved surfaces.

Can you change the layout of your landscape to reduce runoff?

An essential part of stormwater management is keeping water from leaving your property, or at least slowing its flow as much as possible. Many home lawns are sloped to encourage water to run off onto neighboring property or streets. Instead, you could provide low areas landscaped with shrubs and flowers to encourage water to soak into the ground. If your yard is hilly, you can terrace slopes to slow the flow of runoff and make mowing and gardening easier. If you have a large lot, consider "naturalizing" areas with prairie, woodland, or wetland plants. If your property adjoins a lake or stream, one of the best ways to slow and filter runoff is to leave a buffer strip of thick vegetation along the waterfront (figure 2.5). Good sources for ideas are your local Cooperative Extension, Natural Resources Conservation Service, or soil and water conservation district offices.

Assessment 2 — Landscaping and site management to control runoff

For each question in the assessment table on the following page, indicate your risk level in the right-hand column. Select the answer that best matches your situation. Refer to part 2 above if you need more information to complete the table.

Responding to risks

As before, your goal is to lower your risks. In the action checklist on page 22, record your medium- and high-risk practices. Use the recommendations in part 2 to help reduce your risks.

ACTION CHECKLIST

Go back over the assessment tables to ensure that all medium and high risks you identified are recorded in the checklist on page 22. For each medium and high risk, write down the improvements you plan to make. Use recommendations from this chapter and other resources to decide on actions you are likely to complete. A target date will keep you on schedule. You don't have to do everything at once, but try to eliminate the most serious risks as soon as you can. Often it helps to tackle the inexpensive actions first.

For More Information

Contact your local Cooperative Extension office or state department of natural/environmental resources for information on landscaping, nonpoint source pollution, and stormwater management techniques.

Resources and publications

Bay Book: A Guide to Reducing Water Pollution at Home (1993). Available from the Chesapeake Regional Information Service (CRIS), a project of the Alliance for the Chesapeake Bay, 6600 York Road, Baltimore, MD 21212; (800) 662-2747.

Mowing up to the streambank increases rainfall runoff into the stream.

Figure 2.5 To help prevent erosion, leave an unmowed buffer strip of thick vegetation along streambanks and lakeshores.

	LOW RISK	MEDIUM RISK	HIGH RISK	YOUR RISK
Bare soil in lawns and gardens	Bare spots in the lawn are promptly seeded and topped with a layer of straw or mulch. Bare soil in gardens is covered with mulch.	Grass or other ground cover is spotty, particularly on slopes.	Spots in the lawn or garden are left without mulch or vegetation for long periods.	❒ Low ❒ Medium ❒ High
Bare soil during construction	Bare soil is seeded and mulched as soon as possible (before construction is completed). Sediment barriers are used until grass covers soil.	Soil is left bare until construction is completed. Sediment barriers are installed and maintained to detain muddy runoff until grass covers soil.	Soil is left bare and no sediment barriers are used.	❒ Low ❒ Medium ❒ High
Paved surfaces	Paved surfaces are minimized. Alternatives such as wood chips or paving blocks are used for walkways, patios, and other areas.	Some small areas are paved for patios or basketball.	Paved surfaces are used extensively.	❒ Low ❒ Medium ❒ High
Basement protection	Stormwater is diverted from basement windows by window well covers and other devices. Yard is sloped away from the foundation. Downspouts direct roof drainage away from the house.	No special water diversion methods are installed, but stormwater has never entered the basement.	No water diversion methods are attempted. Stormwater runoff has entered the basement or flows near the foundation.	❒ Low ❒ Medium ❒ High
Roof drainage	Downspouts and drip lines direct roof drainage onto a lawn or garden where water soaks into the ground.	Some downspouts and drip lines discharge water onto paved surfaces or grassy areas where water runs off.	Most or all drip lines or downspouts discharge onto paved surfaces, or downspouts are connected directly to storm drains.	❒ Low ❒ Medium ❒ High
Landscaping and buffer strips	Yard is landscaped to slow the flow of stormwater and provide areas where water soaks into the ground. Unmowed buffer strips of thick vegetation are left along streams or lakeshores.	No areas are landscaped to encourage water to soak in, but yard is relatively flat and little runoff occurs. Mowed grass or spotty vegetation exists adjacent to a stream or lake.	There is no landscaping to slow the flow of stormwater, especially on hilly, erodible properties. Stream banks or lakeshores are eroding.	❒ Low ❒ Medium ❒ High

The following stormwater-related publications are available from the University of Wisconsin–Extension Publications, Room 170, 630 West Mifflin Street, Madison, WI 53703-2636; (608) 262-3346. Up to five copies are free; call for price information if you want more than five copies.

- Storm Sewers: The Rivers Beneath Our Feet (GWQ004)
- Cleaning Up Stormwater Runoff (GWQ016)
- Beneficial Landscape Practices (GWQ008)
- Car Care for Cleaner Water (GWQ019)
- Lawn and Garden Fertilizers (GWQ002)
- Shoreline Plants and Landscaping (GWQ014)
- Lawn and Garden Pesticides (GWQ011)
- Lawn Watering (GWQ012)
- Pet Waste and Water Quality (GWQ006)
- Practical Tips for Home and Yard (GWQ007)

► ACTION CHECKLIST ◄
Stormwater Management

Write all high and medium risks below.	What can you do to reduce the risk?	Set a target date for action.
Sample: Pet wastes left in areas where runoff occurs.	Bury wastes away from gardens, wells, ditches, or areas where children play.	One week from today: April 8

*Home*A*Syst* Helps Ensure Your Safety

This *Home*A*Syst* handbook covers a variety of topics to help homeowners examine and address their most important environmental concerns. See the complete list of chapters in the table of contents at the beginning of this handbook. For more information about topics covered in *Home*A*Syst*, or for information about laws and regulations specific to your area, contact your nearest Cooperative Extension office.

Contact the National Farm*A*Syst/Home*A*Syst Office at: B142 Steenbock Library, 550 Babcock Drive, Madison, WI 53706-1293; phone: (608) 262-0024; e-mail: <HOMEASYST@MACC.WISC.EDU>.

This chapter was written by Carl DuPoldt, Environmental Engineer, Natural Resources Conservation Service, Somerset, New Jersey and Carolyn Johnson, Water Quality Education Specialist, University of Wisconsin Cooperative Extension, Milwaukee.

Chapter 3

DRINKING WATER WELL MANAGEMENT

by Bill McGowan, University of Delaware Cooperative Extension

Keeping your well water free of harmful contaminants is a top priority — for your health and for the environment. This chapter helps you examine how you manage your well, and how activities on or near your property may affect well water quality. The following topics are covered:

1. *Well Location.* How close is your well to potential pollution sources? How might your soil type affect water quality?

2. *Well Construction and Maintenance.* Do you know how old your well is and what type of well it is? Is your well casing properly sealed?

3. *Water Testing and Unused Wells.* Have tests of your well water revealed any problems? Are abandoned wells protected against contamination?

Why should you be concerned?

About 95% of rural residents use private wells to supply drinking water. These wells, which tap into local groundwater, are designed to provide clean, safe drinking water. However, improperly constructed or poorly maintained wells can create a pathway for fertilizers, bacteria, pesticides, or other materials to enter the water supply. Once in groundwater, contaminants can flow from your property to a neighbor's well, or from a neighbor's property to *your* well.

Contaminants often have no odor or color and therefore are hard to detect. They can put your health at risk, and it is difficult and expensive to remove them. Once your water becomes contaminated, the only options may be to treat your water after pumping, drill a new well, or get your water from another source.

How will this chapter help you protect your drinking water and home environment?

This chapter is a guide to help you better understand the condition of your well and how you take care of it. Easy-to-understand assessment tables help you identify situations and practices that are safe as well as ones that may require prompt attention. Some rural residents use water sources such as lakes, rivers, or cisterns for their drinking water. Additional information on how to safeguard all water sources may be sought from local Cooperative Extension offices, soil and water conservation district staff, state and federal environmental agencies, and the library.

PART 1 — Well Location

Your well's location in relation to other features on or near your property will determine some pollution risks. The nearness of your well to sources of pollution and the direction of groundwater flow between the pollution sources and your well are the primary concerns. At the end of part 1, fill out the assessment table to determine your possible risks. The information below will help you answer questions in the table.

What pollution sources might reach your well?

Whether groundwater in your area is just below the surface or hundreds of feet down, the location of your well on the land surface is very important. Installing a well in a safe place takes careful planning and consideration. Where the well is located in relation to potential pollution sources is a critical factor.

When possible, locate a well where surface water (stormwater runoff, for example) drains away from it. If a well is downhill from a leaking fuel storage tank, septic system, or overfertilized farm field, it runs a greater risk of becoming contaminated than a well on the uphill side of these pollution sources. In areas where the water table is near the surface, groundwater often flows in the same direction as surface water. Surface slope, however, is not always an indicator of groundwater flow.

Changing the location or depth of your well may protect your water supply, but not the groundwater itself. Any condition likely to cause groundwater contamination should be eliminated, even if your well is far removed from the potential source.

Does your well meet separation distance requirements?

Most states require that new wells be located a minimum distance from sources of potential pollution (figure 3.1). When no distances are specified by state or local law, provide as much separation as possible between your well and any potential pollution source — at least 100 feet. Separating your well from a pollution source may reduce the chance of contamination, but it does not guarantee that the well will be safe.

What's underground — soil and bedrock type, distance to the water table?

Pollution risks are greater when the water table is near the surface, because contaminants do not have far to travel. Groundwater contamination is more likely if soils are shallow (a few feet above bedrock) or if they are highly porous (sandy or gravelly). If bedrock below the soil is fractured — that is, if it has many cracks that allow water to seep down rapidly — then groundwater contamination is more likely. Check with neighbors, local farmers, or well drilling companies to learn more about what's under your property. For more information on soil type, bedrock, and the water table, see chapter 1, part 1, "Physical Characteristics of Your Homesite," which begins on page 9.

Assessment 1 — Well location

Use the table at right to rate your well location risks. For each question, indicate your risk level in the right-hand column. Although some choices may not correspond exactly to your situation, choose the response that best fits. Refer to part 1 above if you need more information to complete the table.

Responding to risks

Your goal is to lower your risks. Turn to the action checklist on page 32 to record the medium- and high-risk practices you identified. Use the recommendations above to help you plan actions to reduce your risks.

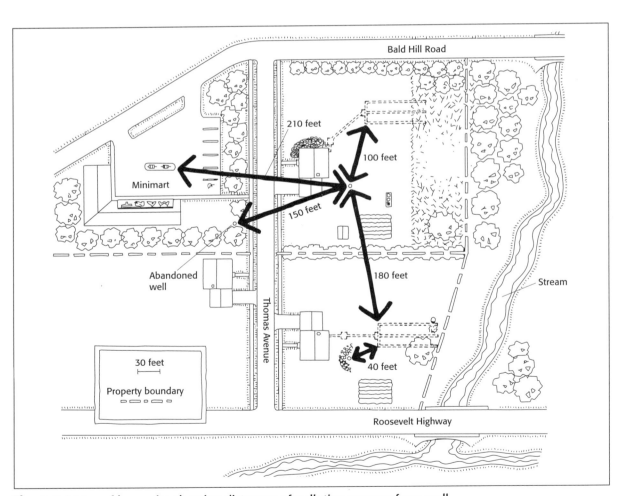

Figure 3.1 Map of homesite showing distances of pollution sources from well.

	LOW RISK	MEDIUM RISK	HIGH RISK	YOUR RISK
Position of well in relation to pollution sources	Well is uphill from all pollution sources. Surface water doesn't reach well or is diverted.	Well is level with or uphill from most pollution sources. Some surface water runoff may reach well.	Well is downhill from pollution sources or in a pit or depression. Surface water runoff reaches well.	❑ Low ❑ Medium ❑ High
Separation distances between well and pollution sources*	Distances from potential pollution sources meet or exceed all state minimum requirements.	Some but not all distances from potential pollution sources meet state minimum requirements.	Distances from most or all potential pollution sources do not meet state minimum requirements.	❑ Low ❑ Medium ❑ High
Soil type	Soil is fine-textured like clay loams or silty clay.	Soil is medium-textured like silt or loam.	Soil is coarse-textured like sand, sandy loam, or gravel.	❑ Low ❑ Medium ❑ High
Subsurface conditions	The water table or fractured bedrock are deeper than 20 feet.	The water table or fractured bedrock are deeper than 20 feet.	The water table or fractured bedrock are shallower than 20 feet.	❑ Low ❑ Medium ❑ High

* Suggested minimum separation distance is 100 feet.

PART 2 — Well Construction and Maintenance

Old or poorly designed wells increase the risk of groundwater contamination by allowing rain or snowmelt to reach the water table without being filtered through soil. If a well is located in a depression or pit or is not properly sealed and capped, surface water carrying nitrates, bacteria, pesticides, and other pollutants may easily contaminate drinking water.

You wouldn't let a car go too long without a tune-up or oil change. Your well deserves the same attention. Good maintenance means keeping the well area clean and accessible, keeping pollutants as far away as possible, and having a qualified well driller or pump installer check the well periodically or when problems are suspected. At the end of part 2, fill out the assessment table to determine risks related to your well's design or condition.

How old is your well?

Well age is an important factor in predicting the likelihood of contamination. Wells constructed more than fifty years ago are likely to be shallow and poorly constructed. Older well pumps are more likely to leak lubricating oils, which can get into the water. Older wells are also more likely to have thinner casings that may be cracked or corroded. Even wells with modern casings that are thirty to forty years old are subject to corrosion and perforation. If you have an older well, you may want to have it inspected by a qualified well driller. If you don't know how old your well is, assume it needs an inspection.

What type of well do you have?

A **dug well** is a large-diameter hole that is usually more than 2 feet wide and often constructed by hand. Dug wells are usually shallow and poorly protected from surface water runoff. **Driven-point (sand-point) wells**, which pose a moderate to high risk, are constructed by driving lengths of pipe into the ground. These wells are normally around 2 inches in diameter and less than 25 feet deep and can only be installed in areas with loose soils such as sand. Most other types of wells are **drilled wells** which, for residential use, are commonly 4 to 8 inches in diameter. Figure 3.2 on the following page shows a properly constructed drilled well.

Are your well casing and well cap protecting your water?

Well drillers install a steel or plastic pipe "casing" to prevent collapse of the well hole during drilling. The space between the casing and sides of the hole is a direct channel for surface water—and pollutants—to reach the water table (figure 3.3 on the following page). To seal off that channel, drillers fill the space with grout (cement or a type of clay called *bentonite*).

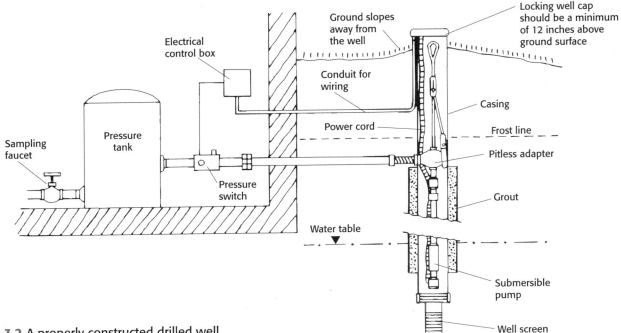

Figure 3.2 A properly constructed drilled well.

You should visually inspect the condition of your well casing for holes or cracks. Examine the part that extends up out of the ground. Remove the cap and inspect inside the casing using a flashlight. If you can move the casing around by pushing it, you may have a problem with your well casing's ability to keep out contaminants. Sometimes damaged casings can be detected by listening for water running down into the well when the pump is not running. If you hear water, there might be a crack in the casing, or the casing may not reach the water table. Either situation is risky.

The depth of casing required for your well depends on the depth to groundwater and the nature of the soils and bedrock below. In sand and gravel soils, well casings should extend to a depth of at least 20 feet and should reach the water table. For wells in bedrock, the casing should extend through the weathered zone and into at least 10 feet of bedrock. A minimum of 20 feet of casing should be used for all wells.

The casing should extend at least 12 inches above the ground surface. If there are occasional floods in your area, the casing should extend 1 to 2 feet above the highest flood level recorded for the site. The ground around the casing should slope away from the wellhead in all directions to prevent water from pooling around the casing.

The well cap should be firmly attached to the casing, with a vent that allows only air to enter. If your well has a vent, be sure that it faces the ground, is tightly connected to the well cap or seal, and is properly screened to keep insects out. Wiring for the pump should be secured in an electric conduit pipe.

Is your well shallow or deep?

As rain and surface water soak into the soil, they may carry pollutants down to the water table. Local geologic conditions determine how long this takes. In some places, the process happens quickly — in weeks, days, or even hours. Shallow wells, which draw from groundwater nearest the land surface, are most likely to be affected by local sources of contamination.

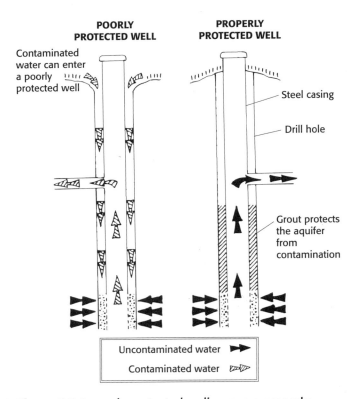

Figure 3.3 A poorly protected well versus a properly protected well.

Do you take measures to prevent backflow?

Backflow of contaminated water into your water supply can occur if your system undergoes sudden pressure loss. Pressure loss can occur if the well fails or, if you are on a public water system, if there is a line break in the system. The simplest way to guard against backflow is to leave an air gap between the water supply line and any reservoir of "dirty" water. For example, if you are filling a swimming pool with a hose, make sure that you leave an air gap between the hose and the water in the pool. Toilets and washing machines have built-in air gaps.

Where an air gap cannot be maintained, a backflow prevention device such a check valve or vacuum breaker should be installed on the water supply line. For example, if you are using a pesticide sprayer that attaches directly to a hose, a check valve should be installed on the faucet to which the hose is connected.

Inexpensive backflow prevention devices can be purchased from plumbing suppliers.

How long since your well was inspected?

Well equipment doesn't last forever. Every ten to fifteen years, your well will require inspection by a qualified well driller or pump installer. You should keep well construction details, as well as the dates and results of maintenance visits for the well and pump. It is important to keep good records so you and future owners can follow a good maintenance schedule.

Assessment 2 — Well construction and maintenance

Use the table below to rate your risks related to well construction and maintenance. For each question, indicate your risk level in the right-hand column. Although some choices may not correspond exactly to your situation, choose the response that best fits. Refer to part 2 above if you need more information.

▶ **ASSESSMENT 2 — Well Construction and Maintenance**

	LOW RISK	MEDIUM RISK	HIGH RISK	YOUR RISK
Well age	Well is less than 20 years old.	Well is 20–50 years old.	Well is more than 50 years old.	❒ Low ❒ Medium ❒ High
Well type	Drilled well.	Driven-point (sand-point) well.	Dug well.	❒ Low ❒ Medium ❒ High
Casing height above land surface	Casing is 12 or more inches above the surface. If the area floods, casing is 1–2 feet above the highest recorded flood level.	Casing is at the surface or up to 12 inches above the surface.	Casing is below the surface or in a pit or basement.	❒ Low ❒ Medium ❒ High
Condition of casing and well cap (seal)	No holes or cracks are visible. Cap is tightly attached. A screened vent faces the ground.	No holes or cracks are visible. Cap is loose.	Holes or cracks are visible. Cap is loose or missing. Running water can be heard or seen.	❒ Low ❒ Medium ❒ High
Casing depth relative to land surface	Casing extends 50 or more feet below the land surface.	Casing extends 20–50 feet below the land surface.	Casing extends less than 20 feet below the land surface.	❒ Low ❒ Medium ❒ High
Backflow protection	Measures are taken to prevent backflow and, where necessary, anti-backflow devices are installed.	Measures are sometimes taken to prevent backflow. No anti-backflow devices are installed.	No measures are taken to prevent backflow. No anti-backflow devices are installed.	❒ Low ❒ Medium ❒ High
Well inspection and "tune-up"	Well was inspected within the last 10 years.	Well was inspected 10–20 years ago.	Well was inspected over 20 years ago or don't know when well was last inspected.	❒ Low ❒ Medium ❒ High

Responding to risks

Your goal is to lower your risks. Turn to the action checklist on page 32 to record the medium- and high-risk practices you identified. Use the recommendations above to help you plan actions to reduce your risks.

PART 3 — Water Testing and Unused Wells

Water testing helps you monitor water quality and identify potential risks to your health. Contaminants enter drinking water from many sources. Many contaminants can only be detected through a water test.

Abandoned wells, if improperly sealed, can provide a direct route for contaminants to enter groundwater. It is important to identify old or abandoned wells and determine appropriate action. At the end of part 3, fill out the assessment table to determine water quality risks related to water contaminants and old wells.

Are there any unused and abandoned wells on your property?

Many properties have wells that are no longer used. Sites with older homes often have an abandoned shallow well that was installed when the house was first built. If not properly filled and sealed, these wells can provide a direct channel for waterborne pollutants to reach groundwater (figure 3.4).

A licensed, registered well driller or pump installer should be hired to close these wells. Effective well plugging calls for experience with well construction materials and methods, as well as knowledge of the geology of the site. The cost to close a well will vary with well depth, well diameter, and soil/rock type. The money spent sealing a well will be a bargain compared to the potential costs of cleanup or the loss of property value if contamination occurs.

When was your water last tested?

At a minimum, your water should be tested *every year* for the four most common indicators of trouble: bacteria, nitrates, pH, and total dissolved solids (TDS). If you haven't had a full-spectrum, comprehensive water test, then you don't know the characteristics of your water. Figure 3.5 shows the general procedure for taking a water sample. Always follow lab instructions.

A more complete water analysis for a private well will tell you about its hardness; corrosivity; and iron, sodium, and chloride content. In addition, you may choose to obtain a broad-scan test of your water for other contaminants such as pesticides. A good source of information on well water quality may be your neighbors. Ask them what their tests have revealed.

What contaminants should you look for?

Test for the contaminants that might be found at your location. For example, if you have lead pipes, soldered copper joints, or brass parts in the pump, test for the presence of lead. Test for volatile organic chemicals (VOCs) if there has been a nearby use or spill of oil, liquid fuels, or solvents. Figure 3.6 (page 30) shows

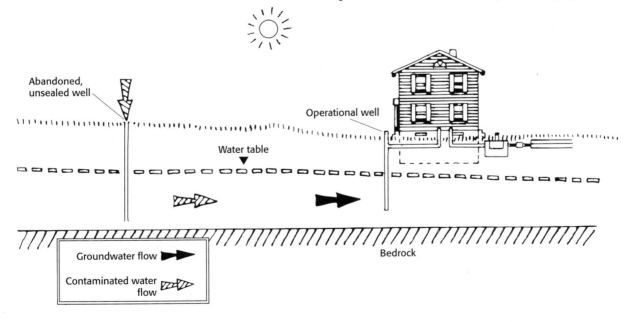

Figure 3.4 Abandoned wells that are not properly sealed provide a pathway for contaminants to reach groundwater.

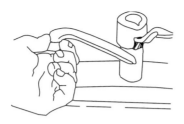

STEP 1: Remove the aerator from an indoor, leak-free cold water faucet. If testing for bacteria, flame the end of the faucet with a lighter. (*Note:* Flaming may discolor chrome or gold-finished faucets.)

STEP 2: Let water run for five minutes to bring in water that has not been in contact with household plumbing. (Skip this step if testing for corrosion of household plumbing—see notes.)

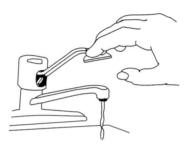

STEP 3: Reduce the water flow until the stream is about ¼-inch in diameter.

STEP 4: Fill a specially prepared laboratory container as instructed by the laboratory. Do not let anything touch the inside of the cap or container.

STEP 5: Close the sample container and transport it as instructed by the laboratory.

Notes:
- Corrosive water may dissolve lead, copper, zinc, or iron contained in household plumbing. If testing for evidence of corrosion, let water stand in the plumbing system at least 12 hours.
- Laboratories specially prepare containers for each category of contaminant. Do not rinse laboratory containers or fill them to overflowing.
- Always follow laboratory directions.

Figure 3.5 Generalized procedure for collecting water samples.

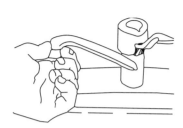

STEP 1: Remove the aerator from an indoor, leak-free cold water faucet.

STEP 2: Let water run for five minutes to bring in water that has not been in contact with household plumbing.

STEP 3: Reduce the water flow until the stream is about ¼-inch in diameter.

STEP 4: Fill a specially prepared laboratory container as instructed by the laboratory. Hold the container at an angle to reduce aeration.

STEP 5: Fill the container until a positive meniscus forms.

STEP 6: Replace the cap. Avoid trapping air between the sample and the cap.

STEP 7: Turn the vial upside down and tap. If bubbles appear, take another sample. If not, transport the container as instructed by the laboratory.

Notes:
- Laboratories specially prepare containers for each category of contaminant. Do not rinse laboratory containers or fill them to overflowing.
- Always follow laboratory directions.

Figure 3.6 Generalized procedure for collecting water samples if testing for volatile organic chemicals (VOCs).

the general procedure for collecting a water sample if testing for VOCs. Always follow lab instructions when taking a water sample.

Pesticide tests, though expensive, may be justified if your well has high nitrate levels — more than 10 milligrams per liter (mg/l) of nitrate-nitrogen (NO_3–N) or 45 mg/l of nitrate (NO_3). Tests are also warranted if a pesticide spill has occurred near the well. Pesticides are more likely to be a problem if your well is shallow, has less than 15 feet of casing below the water table, or is located in sandy soil and is downslope from irrigated lands such as farms or golf courses where pesticides are used.

You can seek further advice on testing from your local Cooperative Extension office or health department. You should test your water more than once a year if (1) someone in your household is pregnant or nursing; (2) there are unexplained illnesses in the family; (3) your neighbors find a dangerous contaminant in their water; (4) you note a change in water taste, odor, color, or clarity; or (5) you have a spill or back-siphonage of chemicals or fuels into or near your well. Water can be tested by both public and private laboratories. Once tested, keep a record of your results with your records on well construction and maintenance. This will allow you to monitor water quality over time.

Assessment 3 — Water testing and unused wells

Use the table below to rate your risks related to water quality and unused wells. For each question, indicate your risk level in the right-hand column. Although some choices may not correspond exactly to your situation, choose the response that best fits. Refer to part 3 above if you need more information.

Responding to risks

Your goal is to lower your risks. Turn to the action checklist on page 32 to record the medium- and high-risk practices you identified. Use the information above to help you plan actions to reduce your risks.

ACTION CHECKLIST

When you finish the assessment tables, go back over the questions to ensure that every high and medium risk you identified is recorded in the checklist on page 32. For each risk, write down the improvements you plan to make. Use recommendations from this chapter and from resources elsewhere. Pick a target date that will keep you on schedule for making the changes. You don't have to do everything at once, but try to eliminate the most serious risks as soon as you can. Often it helps to start with inexpensive actions.

For More Information

Well construction and maintenance

Private Water Systems Handbook, MWPS–14. A 72-page publication available from the Northeast Regional Agricultural Engineering Service (NRAES). See page 116 for ordering information.

Water testing

Contact your local health department or Cooperative Extension office, private testing laboratories, or a state environmental agency.

Drilling and sealing wells

Contact local plumbers, well drillers, or the government agency that regulates well drilling and health standards.

Groundwater, soil type, and geology

Contact your state or U.S. Geological Survey.

▶ **ASSESSMENT 3 — Water Testing and Unused Wells**

	LOW RISK	MEDIUM RISK	HIGH RISK	YOUR RISK
Water testing	Consistent, good water quality. Tests meet standards for bacteria, nitrate, and other contaminants.	Some tests do not meet standards or tests approach standards.	Water is not tested. Water is discolored after a rainstorm or during spring melt. There are noticeable changes in color, odor, and taste.	❐ Low ❐ Medium ❐ High
Unused wells on your property or in your area	There are no unused wells, or there are unused wells that are properly sealed.	There are unused wells that are not sealed but are capped and isolated from contaminants.	There are unused, unsealed wells that are in poor condition, near pollution sources, and/or uncapped.	❐ Low ❐ Medium ❐ High

► ACTION CHECKLIST ◄
Drinking Water Well Management

Write all high and medium risks below.	What can you do to reduce the risk?	Set a target date for action.
Sample: Water hasn't been tested for 10 years. Smells different than it used to.	Have sample tested in state office of public health.	One week from today: April 8

Drinking water quality standards

Call the U.S. Environmental Protection Agency's Safe Drinking Water Hotline toll-free at (800) 426-4791 from 9:00 A.M. to 5:30 P.M., EST, Monday through Friday.

Home*A*Syst Helps Ensure Your Safety

This *Home*A*Syst* handbook covers a variety of topics to help homeowners examine and address their most important environmental concerns. See the complete list of chapters in the table of contents at the beginning of this handbook. For more information about topics covered in *Home*A*Syst,* or for information about laws and regulations specific to your area, contact your nearest Cooperative Extension office.

Contact the National Farm*A*Syst/Home*A*Syst Office at: B142 Steenbock Library, 550 Babcock Drive, Madison, WI 53706-1293; phone: (608) 262-0024; e-mail: <HOMEASYST@MACC.WISC.EDU>.

This chapter was adapted by Bill McGowan, Agriculture/Water Quality Extension Educator, University of Delaware Cooperative Extension. Adapted from Farm*A*Syst fact sheet #1, "Reducing the Risk of Groundwater Contamination by Improving Drinking Water Well Condition," by Susan Jones, U.S. EPA Region V, Water Division, and University of Wisconsin–Cooperative Extension.

Chapter 4

HOUSEHOLD WASTEWATER: Septic Systems and Other Treatment Methods

by Barbara Kneen Avery, College of Human Ecology, Cornell Cooperative Extension

This chapter covers three factors that affect your pollution risks:

1. *Septic System Design and Location.* Topics covered in this section include knowing your septic tank capacity, soil type in the drainfield, and system's location.

2. *On-Site System Maintenance.* Pumping the septic tank, protecting the drainfield, and watching for signs of trouble are discussed in this section.

3. *Septic or Sewage System Inputs.* Reducing the amount of water, solids, and harmful chemicals going into your individual septic or municipal wastewater treatment system is reviewed in this section.

This chapter will help you evaluate your septic system and pinpoint risks before they become problems. It provides general guidelines for safe management of household wastewater. State and local laws, however, may impose more stringent or additional requirements. For example, some systems, such as cesspools, may be banned locally. Contact your nearest Cooperative Extension office, a local health or environmental agency, or a septic system contractor for advice.

Why should you be concerned?

Wastewater treatment systems help protect your health and the environment. Household wastewater from sinks, toilets, washing machines, and showers carries dirt, soap, food, grease, and bodily wastes "down the drain" and out of your house (figure 4.1).

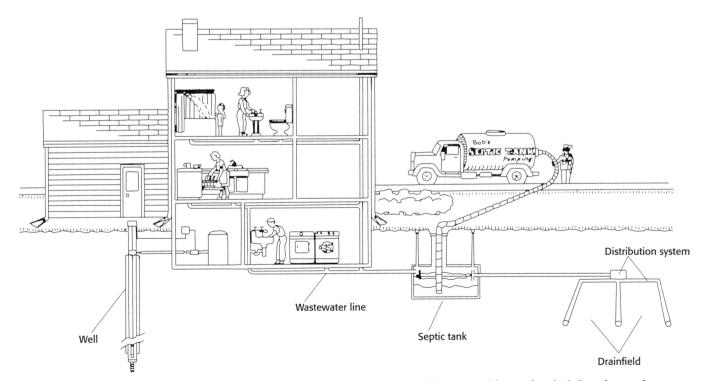

Figure 4.1 Household wastewater carries dirt, soap, food, grease, and bodily wastes "down the drain" and out of your house to an on-site septic or municipal wastewater treatment system.

Wastewater also carries disease-causing bacteria, viruses, and other pathogens as well as nutrients like nitrogen, phosphorus, and organic wastes. Such nutrients promote weed growth and lower oxygen levels in surface water and thus affect fishing and recreational use of rivers and lakes.

Wastewater treatment systems are designed to remove or break down these contaminants before they enter groundwater—the source of drinking water via wells—or nearby lakes, streams, or wetlands.

Wastewater treatment is often out-of-sight and out-of-mind until problems occur. Knowing the basics about your household system and taking simple precautions can prevent problems. It's a wise investment to keep your system working well. Replacing a failed system can cost thousands of dollars.

Where is your wastewater treated?

Do you have a septic system or other on-site system to treat wastewater?

This chapter is geared primarily toward homeowners or tenants who have septic systems buried in their yards. A typical septic system consists of a septic tank and drainfield, which is also known as a soil absorption field, leach field, or tile field (see figure 4.1 on the previous page). It is important to maintain your wastewater treatment system and use it wisely whether you have a holding tank or septic tank followed by a mound, sand filter, or other alternative on-site treatment system. (These types of systems are discussed further on the following pages.)

Are you hooked up to a city or community sewer system?

Even if wastewater is not treated on your home site, there are still ways you can reduce the impact your wastewater has on your community and the environment. Conserving water and being careful about what you put down the drain are easy ways to help (this is discussed in part 3 of this chapter). Using your municipal sewage treatment system wisely saves taxpayers' dollars and protects our water resources.

How does a conventional septic system work?

First, wastewater flows through a sewer pipe out of your house and into the septic tank, a box or cylinder commonly made out of

concrete (figure 4.2). Fiberglass and polyethylene tanks are also used. The tank must be watertight to keep sewage from leaking out and groundwater from seeping in.

Lighter solids in the wastewater—like grease, hair, and soap—float to the top of the tank and form a scum layer. Heavier solids settle to the bottom and form a layer of sludge. Bacteria in the tank begin to break down some of the sludge into simple nutrients, gas, and water. The remaining solids are stored in the tank until they are pumped out. A baffle or a sanitary tee pipe at the tank inlet slows the incoming rush of water, so the sludge is not stirred up. A baffle or a sanitary tee pipe located at the tank's outlet keeps solids from leaving the tank. Inspection pipes at the top of the tank are for inspecting the inlet and outlet pipes, baffles, and tee pipes.

Next, the liquid waste, or effluent, flows out of the tank, through the distribution system, and into the drainfield or soil absorption field (figure 4.3). The distribution system consists of a series of perforated plastic distribution pipes or concrete galleys laid in the ground, usually in gravel-filled trenches. Effluent can be fed into the pipes by gravity or by a pump. The effluent moves slowly out of the trench and is absorbed into the soil. An effluent filter at the tank outlet is recommended, because particles carried out of the septic tank can clog the drainfield.

The soil must be of a suitable type and deep enough to treat wastewater before it reaches groundwater. The soil filters out larger particles and pathogens, which eventually die off in the inhospitable soil environment. Under suitable conditions, beneficial soil microbes and natural chemical processes break down or remove

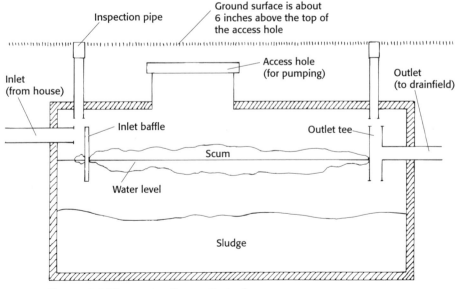

Figure 4.2 The parts of a septic tank.

most of the contaminants in the effluent. Hazardous synthetic chemicals such as solvents and fuels are not easily degraded in wastewater treatment systems. These chemicals can contaminate sludge in the septic tank, kill the beneficial bacteria that digest wastes, and travel into groundwater.

Soils vary in their ability to absorb and treat wastewater. Well-drained, medium-textured soils such as loam are best. Coarse gravel or sandy soils allow wastewater to flow too quickly for treatment. In fine clay or compacted soils, water moves too slowly. Soil microbes need oxygen to digest wastes quickly. If the air spaces between soil particles remain filled with water, the lack of oxygen prevents the rapid breakdown of wastes by aerobic (oxygen-requiring) soil microbes.

Anaerobic soil microbes (those that live in the absence of oxygen) digest wastes slowly and give off putrid, smelly gases characteristic of a failing septic system. Anaerobic conditions occur when soils are poorly drained, groundwater levels are high, surface runoff saturates the drainfield, or excessive amounts of water are used in your household.

Good wastewater treatment depends on good dispersal of wastewater over the drainfield. In a conventional, gravity-fed distribution system, the distribution pipes are often laid out in a fork-shaped pattern joined by a distribution box (figure 4.3). Leveling devices on the distribution box help ensure an even flow of wastewater to every trench. Often, however, certain trenches or low points in the distribution system receive more effluent than others.

A dosing or enhanced-flow system has a pump or siphon to improve the distribution of effluent. Periodically pumping a certain volume of effluent to wet the entire drainfield area and then allowing the soil to drain between doses provides a period of aeration, which helps microorganisms in the soil digest the wastes.

In a pressure distribution system, effluent is pumped directly through small-diameter pipes, not sent through a distribution box. Wastewater is evenly distributed throughout the entire drainfield, promoting better treatment of wastewater and system longevity.

Alternating trenches are another means of providing a period of aeration (figure 4.4 on the following page). Adjusting the outlet levels or using a plug or valve in the distribution box allows effluent to flow into only some of the trenches while other trenches are allowed to rest for about six months. A serial distribution system is designed so that the trenches are used in sequence; when the first trench is overloaded, the wastewater overflows into the next trench downslope.

Seepage pits and cesspools are perforated tanks or pits lined with concrete blocks or bricks through which wastewater can seep into the ground. They are usually less effective than other soil absorption systems because they are located closer to the water table than trenches and often lack sufficient soil surface area for

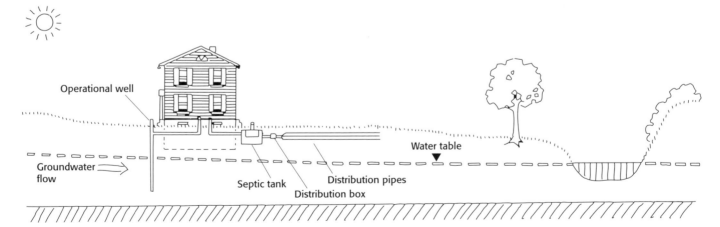

Figure 4.3 Cross section of a septic system showing the septic tank and distribution system.

good wastewater treatment. Without a septic tank for pretreatment, a cesspool has the added problem of sludge accumulation in the pit. Cesspools are banned in some states.

What are some alternative systems?

If soil or site conditions are not suitable for a conventional drainfield, an alternative system might be used. In a mound system, the drainfield is elevated to provide additional soil depth for treatment before the effluent reaches groundwater (figure 4.5 on the following page). A sand filter consists of layers of sand and gravel in which the wastewater is treated before it is distributed into the soil. Other types of filters use small foam pieces or peat as a filter medium.

With suitable climate and soil conditions, other alternative systems such as evapotranspiration systems, constructed wetlands, spray irrigation, lagoons, or mechanically aerated systems for household wastewater treatment are approved in some localities. Descriptions of these systems are beyond the scope of this publication; please see "For More Information" beginning on page 44 for additional resources.

Aerobic treatment units operate much like a municipal sewage treatment plant, where wastewater is mixed with air, promoting bacterial digestion of organic wastes and pathogens. The biological breakdown of wastes in a septic tank's anaerobic (oxygen-deprived) conditions is relatively slow. Aerobic units are more expensive and require significantly more maintenance than conventional septic tanks. However, they provide good wastewater treatment on homesites that are otherwise unsuitable for development because the soil type, depth, or area is inadequate for an on-site treatment system. The effluent from an aerobic unit can be discharged into a soil absorption system or may be treated with chlorine, ozone, or other disinfectant before surface discharge if state and local regulations permit.

Holding tanks may be used in temporary situations such as when you are awaiting a new system hookup or at a summer residence. Unlike a septic tank, a holding tank has no outlet and must be pumped frequently to take the wastewater to a treatment facility.

Disposal of toilet wastes does not have to mean flushing away great volumes of water. Composting toilets use microbes to aerobically digest toilet wastes; they work well only if the right temperature, moisture level, oxygen level, and nutrient mixture is maintained. Other types of waterless toilets include incinerating toilets, recirculating oil-flush toilets, and chemical disinfecting toilets. Without the blackwater (water carrying human body waste) from toilets, greywater (wastewater other than sewage) from sinks, tubs, and washing machines can be treated in a household wastewater system sized to handle about half the volume of a standard wastewater system.

There is controversy over the safe use and disposal of greywater: state health regulations covering if and how greywater can be used vary. Many states strictly prohibit any surface disposal of greywater but permit its use in subsurface irrigation systems for watering plants. However, caution is advised because greywater may contain infectious bacteria and viruses (for example, from soiled diapers or clothing worn by someone with an infectious disease). Direct contact with greywater must be prevented. Beware that certain detergents, bleach, and salts may damage the health of plants and soils.

In areas with limited water resources, particularly during drought periods, water use must be reduced. Water conservation methods (see page 43 for suggestions) are encouraged, along with unrestricted uses of clear water (for example, flushing toilets with shower warm-up water).

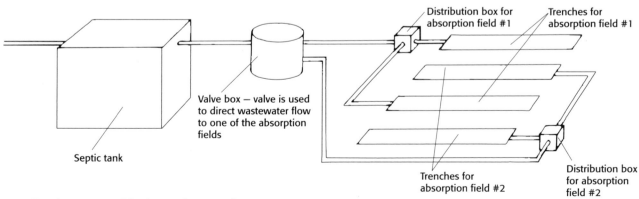

Figure 4.4 Septic system with alternating trenches.

PART 1 — Septic System Design and Location

How much wastewater can your system handle?

Both the septic tank and drainfield should have adequate capacity to treat all the wastewater generated in your house, even at times of peak use. The system must be designed for the maximum occupancy of your home. The amount of wastewater flowing out of a house is an estimated 100 to 200 gallons per bedroom per day multiplied by the number of bedrooms in the home. Each state sets procedures for calculating wastewater flow and sizing on-site treatment systems. Installing low-flow toilets and water-saving faucets will reduce the size of the system needed.

The septic tank should be large enough to hold two days' worth of wastewater. (Two days is long enough to allow solids to settle out by gravity.) Typically, a new three-bedroom home is equipped with a 1,000-gallon tank. A two-compartment tank or a second tank in series can improve sludge and scum removal and help prevent drainfield clogging.

The required length of the drainfield trenches is based on how much wastewater will be put in the system and how much water a unit area of soil can treat. The better the soil type or longer the trenches, the higher the system's capacity for wastewater treatment. Contact your home contractor, septic system installer, local health department, or environmental agency for information they may have on file about your septic system age, design, and location.

Water use in your household in excess of the system's design capacity leads to inadequate wastewater treatment or system failure. Conserving water or more fre-

---

IS YOUR SEPTIC TANK CAPACITY ADEQUATE?

Water usage in the United States ranges from 50 to 100 gallons per day (gpd) per person. Estimate the wastewater load from your household using the equation below. Your septic tank should be able to hold two days' worth of wastewater.

_____ people in household x 75 gpd (average) =

_____ gpd x 2 days = _____ gallons

What is your septic tank capacity? _____ gallons
(If you don't know, ask your tank installer or pumper.)

Is your tank size adequate for your present household size? Yes   No

Calculate the wastewater load from your home if each bedroom were occupied by two people:

_____ bedrooms x 150 gpd = _____ gpd x 2 days =

_____ gallons

This is the recommended tank size for your home if each bedroom were occupied by two people.

Would your septic tank capacity be adequate if each bedroom were occupied by two people? Yes   No

---

quent pumping may extend the life of the system. The addition of a bathroom, bedroom, or water-using appliance (such as a Jacuzzi, dishwasher, or water softener) to your home may require expanding your system. The use of former vacation cottages as permanent dwellings or as heavily used vacation rentals may render an existing system inadequate. Several teen-

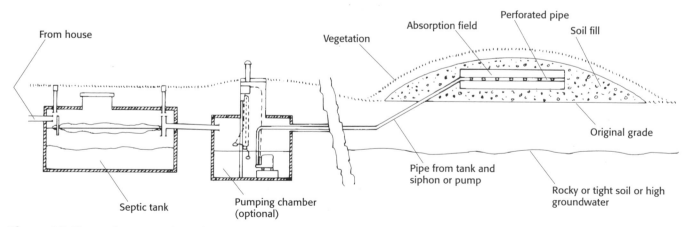

Figure 4.5 Alternative mound septic system.

agers living in a house may overload the system's capacity.

How close is too close?

To prevent contamination of water supplies, the drainfield must be at least 100 feet from any wetland, shoreline, stream bed, or drinking water well (see figure 4.6; state and local regulations regarding separation distances may vary). The greater the distance, the lower the chance of contaminating the water supply. If your system is downhill from a well, the well will be better protected. (If you do not know where your system is located, see part 2 of this chapter.)

You should test your well water more often for nitrates and bacteria if your system is closer to your well than recommended. For information on certified laboratory testing, contact your local Cooperative Extension office or public health agency, or look under "laboratories" or "water" in the yellow pages. Chapter 3 provides more information on well protection.

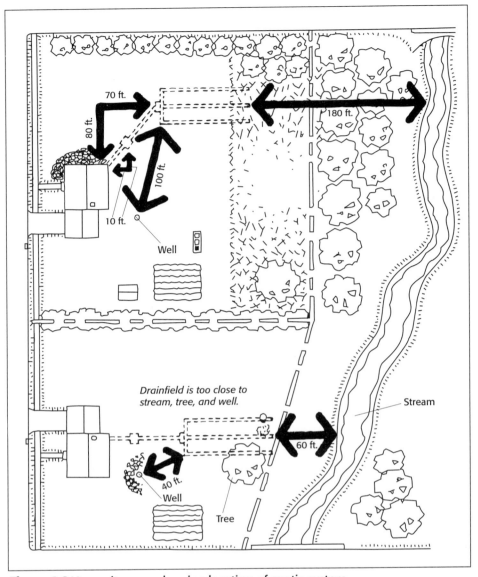

Figure 4.6 Homesite map showing location of septic system.

When was your septic system installed?

Septic systems should last fifteen to forty years or longer, depending on how appropriately they were designed for a site and how well they are maintained. If your septic tank is made of steel, it will rust and need replacement. The older your system, the more likely that it does not meet the latest standards. Even a relatively new system can fail if it is located in poor soil, undersized, or not properly installed or maintained. Look for the signs on failure listed in part 2 of this chapter.

Do you have an effluent filter and gas baffle installed at the septic tank outlet?

Solids that do not settle out in the tank can be carried out of the tank with effluent, clog the drainfield, and lead to premature system failure. Effluent filters on the outlet capture small particles and prevent them from clogging the drainfield; it is important to periodically clean the filter. Gas bubbles are produced by anaerobic bacteria slowly digesting wastes in the tank. A gas baffle near the outlet deflects the bubbles and the disturbed sludge away from the outlet.

Does your system need safety devices?

To prevent hazardous sewage overflows, tanks and chambers should have a storage capacity above normal working levels. In addition, an alarm should be installed on holding tanks or pumping chambers to warn you if the tank is nearly full. If your system depends on a pump (and not gravity), you may need to have a backup power supply available in addition to adequate storage capacity in the tank. In flood hazard areas, backflow valves should be installed on the main distribution line to prevent waste from flooding back into the tank and your home.

Assessment 1 — Septic system design and location

Use the assessment table below to begin rating your risks related to septic system design and location. For each question, mark your risk level in the right-hand column. Although some choices may not correspond exactly to your situation, choose the response that best fits.

Responding to risks

Your goal is to lower the risks. Use the action checklist on page 45 to record medium- and high-risk practices. Use recommendations in part 1 to help you make plans to reduce your risks.

PART 2 — On-Site System Maintenance

Do you know exactly where your system is located?

To take proper care of a septic system, you must know where it is. The exact locations of system components are not obvious, because they are below ground. If the location of your system is not in your home records, then a previous homeowner, county health department, or pumper's records may hold the answer.

You may be able to locate your septic tank yourself. In the basement, look for the sewer pipe leaving the house and note the direction in which it goes through the wall. Then, go outside and probe the ground with a narrow metal rod or dig into the ground 10 to 20 feet away from the house in the direction of the house

▶ **ASSESSMENT 1 — Septic System Design and Location**

	LOW RISK	MEDIUM RISK	HIGH RISK	YOUR RISK
Capacity of system	Tank is designed to handle more wastewater than required, based on the size of the home.	Capacity just meets load requirements, but I watch out for factors indicating system overload. Water conservation measures are taken.	Bathrooms, bedrooms, or water-using appliances are added without reexamining the capacity of the wastewater system.	❐ Low ❐ Medium ❐ High
Separation distance	Drainfield is at least 100 feet from any well or surface water.	Drainfield is between 50 and 100 feet from a well or surface water.	Drainfield is less than 50 feet from a well or surface water.	❐ Low ❐ Medium ❐ High
Age of system or holding tank YEAR INSTALLED:	System is five years old or less.	System is between six and twenty years old.	System is more than twenty years old.	❐ Low ❐ Medium ❐ High
Effluent filter	An effluent filter is installed and cleaned regularly.	An effluent filter is installed but not cleaned often enough.	There is no effluent filter installed on the septic tank outlet.	❐ Low ❐ Medium ❐ High
Safety devices	An alarm on the pumping chamber or holding tank indicates that the tank is full or power has been cut off to the pump.		There is no alarm to indicate tank overflow or that power has been cut off to the pump.	❐ Low ❐ High
Backflow protection	A backflow valve is installed to prevent backup during floods.		No backflow valve is installed to prevent backup during floods.	❐ Low ❐ High

sewer line. The septic tank is usually within 2 feet of the ground surface. The distribution box and drainfield are usually located downslope from the septic tank. In some situations, the wastewater is pumped to a drainfield uphill from the septic tank.

Once you've located the septic tank, sketch a map of your house and yard (chapter 1, "Site Assessment," will get you started on a map). Note the distances from the septic tank opening to at least two permanent points such as the corner of the house foundation or survey stakes on the property line (see figure 4.6 on page 38). As long as the distances are correct, the map doesn't have to be drawn to scale. If known, show the location of the drainfield. Keep the map on file along with other maintenance records and pass it on to subsequent owners of the house.

Do you know when your tank was last pumped or inspected?

Keeping good records each time your septic system is pumped, inspected, or repaired will help you make cost-effective maintenance decisions (see sidebar below). This information will also be valuable if you sell or transfer your property.

How often should your tank be pumped?

Regular pumping is the most important action you can take to maintain your system. As more solids accumulate in the tank, particles are more likely to flow out of the tank and into the drainfield. The cost of pumping a septic tank ($100 to $250) is far less than the expense of replacing a drainfield clogged by escaping solids ($2,000 to $8,000 depending on site conditions and the size of the home).

The best way to determine when to pump your tank is to have it inspected annually. The tank needs to be pumped if (see figure 4.7):

- the sum of the solid layers (sludge plus scum) takes up more than half of the tank capacity,
- the top of the sludge layer is less than a foot below the outlet baffle or tee, or
- the bottom of the scum layer is within three inches of the bottom of the outlet baffle (or top of the outlet tee).

Pumping as needed based on the results of periodic inspections will minimize your maintenance costs and maximize the system's longevity. Inspections can also identify problems with system components before they cause a backup or drainfield failure.

A general rule of thumb is to have a septic tank pumped by a licensed pumper every three to five years. But how often a tank needs to be pumped depends on the size of your tank, the amount of wastewater generated in your household, the amount of solids carried in the wastewater, and the age of the system.

You can estimate how frequently your tank needs to be pumped using the table on the following page. Find your tank size (in gallons) along the left side of the table. Go across the row for your tank size and down the column for the number of people in your home. Where the row and column intersect, you'll find the estimated number of years between pumpings.

After pumping, the tank should also be inspected by a professional for cracks and the condition of the

---

KEEP A MAINTENANCE RECORD

Keeping good records each time your septic system is pumped, inspected, or repaired will help you make cost-effective maintenance decisions.

Date	Work done	Work performed by
May 20	*Installed septic system*	*Installer's name, phone number*

baffles. Leaks should be repaired promptly. Never crawl inside or lean into a septic tank without proper ventilation and safety procedures—**the gases inside the tank can be deadly!**

The distribution box should be periodically checked to be sure that the distribution pipes are properly leveled. Solids accumulating in the distribution box indicate damaged baffles, inadequate septic tank pumping, or that the tank is too small to handle the wastewater load. If the system includes a pump, the pump should be checked along with the float switch, alarm, and air vents to the dosing tank.

A holding tank must be pumped frequently because it has no outlet. Depending on the amount of wastewater generated and tank capacity, you may need to pump it every month or every week. If you assume that every person in the house uses 25 to 75 gallons of water a day, four people can fill a 1,500-gallon tank in five to fifteen days. Overflows are a sure sign that you need to schedule pumping more often.

How can you protect your drainfield?
A septic system depends on good soil conditions for treatment and disposal of effluent. Water must be able to percolate through the soil at a reasonable rate. Some tips for protecting the drainfield are:

- To prevent soil compaction and damage to pipes, do not drive vehicles on the drainfield.

- Do not pave, build, pile logs or other heavy objects, or put a swimming pool over the drainfield. These activities compact the soil, and soil microbes need oxygen to digest wastes.

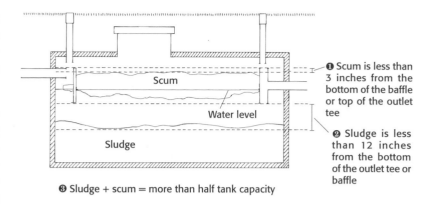

❶ Scum is less than 3 inches from the bottom of the baffle or top of the outlet tee

❷ Sludge is less than 12 inches from the bottom of the outlet tee or baffle

❸ Sludge + scum = more than half tank capacity

Figure 4.7 Three conditions under which a septic tank needs to be pumped.

- Divert roof runoff, footer drains, sump pumps, and other surface runoff away from the drainfield. Saturated soil is less effective at treating wastewater.

- Avoid planting trees and shrubs whose deep roots can damage piping. Grass is the best drainfield cover.

- Install an effluent filter or screen on the septic tank outlet to prevent the carryover of solids into the drainfield.

What are the signs of trouble?
- Foul odors in your home or yard tell you that your system is not working well.

- Slow or backed-up drains may be caused by a clog in the house pipes, septic tank, drainfield, or roof vent for your household plumbing.

- Wet, spongy ground or lush plant growth may appear near a leaky septic tank or failing drainfield.

- Repeated intestinal illnesses in your family may occur if your water is contaminated by poorly treated wastewater. Have your drinking water tested annually for coliform bacteria and nitrates.

- Algal blooms and excessive weed growth in nearby ponds or lakes can be caused by phosphorus leaching from septic systems.

Respond quickly to any problems you observe. You may need to expand or modify your system to avoid further problems. There are many good publications and other resources to help you decide (see "For More Information" beginning on page 44). Call local contractors or visit an extension office to get recommendations.

Try to base your decision on what is best for the environment and your health. Remember, what may seem to be the least expensive option may not be economical in the long run.

ESTIMATED NUMBER OF YEARS BETWEEN SEPTIC TANK PUMPINGS

Tank size (gallons)	Number of people in your household					
	1	2	3	4	5	6
500	5.8	2.6	1.5	1.0	0.7	0.4
1,000	12.4	5.9	3.7	2.6	2.0	1.5
1,500	18.9	9.1	5.9	4.2	3.3	2.6
2,000	25.4	12.4	8.0	5.9	4.5	3.7

Note: More frequent pumping is needed if a garbage disposal is used.
Source: Karen Mancl, "Septic Tank Maintenance," Publication AEX-740, Ohio Cooperative Extension Service, 1988.

Assessment 2 — On-site system maintenance

Use the table below to begin rating your risks related to system maintenance. For each question, indicate your risk level in the right-hand column. Although some choices may not correspond exactly to your situation, choose the response that best fits.

Responding to risks

As always, your goal is to lower your risks. Use the action checklist on page 45 to record your medium- and high-risk practices. Use recommendations in part 2 to help you make plans to reduce your risks.

PART 3 — Septic or Sewage System Inputs

What solid wastes are acceptable?

Your wastewater treatment system is not a substitute for the trash can or a compost pile. Dispose of tissues, diapers, baby wipes, sanitary napkins, tampons, condoms, cigarette butts, and other solid waste with regular garbage and *not* down the toilet. Since these materials do not break down easily, they will cause your septic tank or the settling tanks in a municipal treatment plant to fill up faster.

▶ **ASSESSMENT 2 — On-Site System Maintenance**

	LOW RISK	MEDIUM RISK	HIGH RISK	YOUR RISK
Maps and records	I keep a map and good records of repairs and maintenance.	The location of my tank and date of last pumping are known but not recorded.	The location of my system is unknown. I do not keep a record of pumping and repairs.	❑ Low ❑ Medium ❑ High
Tank pumping (including holding tanks)	The septic tank is pumped on a regular basis as determined by an annual inspection, or about every three to five years. The holding tank is pumped as needed.	The septic tank is pumped, but not regularly.	The septic tank is not pumped. The holding tank overflows or leaks between pumpings.	❑ Low ❑ Medium ❑ High
Condition of tank and baffles	The tank and baffles are inspected for cracks; repairs are made promptly.		The condition of the tank and baffles is unknown.	❑ Low ❑ High
Drainfield protection	Vehicles and other heavy objects or activities are kept from the drainfield area.	Occasionally, the drainfield is compacted by heavy objects or activities.	Vehicles, livestock, heavy objects, or other disturbances are permitted in the drainfield area.	❑ Low ❑ Medium ❑ High
Diverting surface water	All surface runoff is diverted away from the drainfield.	Some surface water flows into the drainfield area.	Runoff from land, rooftops, driveways, etc. flows into the drainfield.	❑ Low ❑ Medium ❑ High
Plantings over the drainfield	Grass or other shallow-rooted plantings are over the drainfield.		Trees and shrubs are growing on or near the drainfield.	❑ Low ❑ High
Signs of trouble	Household drains flow freely. There are no sewage odors inside or outside. Soil over the drainfield is firm and dry. Well water tests negative for coliform bacteria.	Household drains run slowly. Soil over the drainfield is sometimes wet.	Household drains back up. Sewage odors can be noticed in the house or yard. Soil is wet or spongy in the drainfield area. Well water tests positive for coliform bacteria.	❑ Low ❑ Medium ❑ High

Home*A*Syst: An Environmental Risk-Assessment Guide for the Home

Do not use a garbage grinder (dispose-all) in the kitchen sink; it adds to the load on the system. Excess grease, fats, and coffee grounds can clog your system.

Consider composting food waste and even some paper wastes as an alternative. Your local Cooperative Extension office can provide you with information about composting.

What household chemicals can go down the drain?

Wastewater treatment systems are not designed to neutralize the wide variety of common household chemicals. Paints, solvents, acids, drain cleaners, oils, and pesticides can pass untreated through your system and contaminate the groundwater. Though generally safe when diluted, high concentrations or large volumes of water-soluble cleaners or bleach can harm septic tank microbes. See chapter 5, "Managing Hazardous Household Products," for information on the proper disposal of hazardous chemicals.

Chemical products advertised to "sweeten" or improve your septic system operation cannot replace routine pumping and may even be harmful. Buying and adding yeasts, bacteria, or enzymes is not necessary; there are already plenty of the right microbes digesting wastes in your system. Additives containing solvents to unclog your system can kill the microbes needed to digest wastes in your septic tank and drainfield. Furthermore, these solvents may contaminate your drinking water supply.

Why save water?

Average household water usage is shown in the chart at right (figure 4.8). Reducing the flow of wastewater through the septic tank allows more time for solids to settle out and less chance of solid particles being carried over to the drainfield. Less water in the drainfield means better aeration for the soil microbes at work in the system. There are many steps you can take to reduce how much water you use. Here are a few:

- To reduce water consumption by toilets by as much as 50%, install low-flow toilets. Water-saving shower heads and faucets also help. (Low-flow fixtures are *required* in some localities.)
- Take shorter showers.
- Repair leaky faucets and toilets immediately.
- Don't run water longer than necessary; for example, turn the water off while brushing your teeth or shaving.

- Wait until dishwashers and washing machines are full before running a load; scrape but don't pre-rinse dishes before loading them into the dishwasher.
- Adjust water softener settings to reduce the amount of water needed for backwashing and regeneration.
- Spread out laundry and other major water-using chores over the week or day.

Assessment 3 — Septic or sewage system inputs

Use the assessment table on the following page to begin rating your risks relating to system inputs. For each question, indicate your risk level in the right-hand column. Although some choices may not correspond exactly to your situation, choose the response that best fits.

Responding to risks

As always, your goal is to lower your risks. Use the action checklist on page 45 to record your medium- and high-risk practices. Use recommendations in part 3 to help you make plans to reduce your risks.

ACTION CHECKLIST

It is easy to understand how household wastewater systems can be ignored: out of sight, out of mind. But what you do or don't do to maintain your system may affect the health of your family, your neighborhood, or the environment.

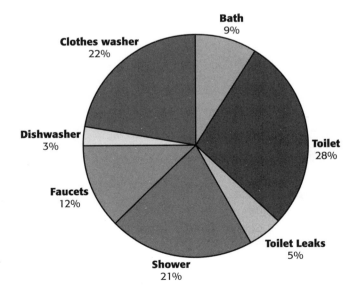

Figure 4.8 Average household water usage.
Source: John Woodwell, "Water Efficiency in Your Home," 1995, Rocky Mountain Institute.

	LOW RISK	MEDIUM RISK	HIGH RISK	YOUR RISK
Solid wastes	There is no garbage grinder (dispose-all) in the kitchen. No grease or coffee grounds are put down the drain. Only toilet tissue is put in the toilet.	There is moderate use of a garbage grinder, and some solids are disposed of down the drain.	There is heavy use of a garbage grinder, and many solids are disposed of down the drain. Many paper products or plastics are flushed down the toilet.	❒ Low ❒ Medium ❒ High
Cleaners, solvents, and other chemicals (also applies to holding tanks)	There is careful use of household chemicals (paints, cleaning products). No solvents, fuels, or other hazardous chemicals are poured down the drain.	There is occasional disposal of hazardous household chemicals in the wastewater system.	There is heavy use of strong cleaning products that end up in wastewater. Hazardous chemicals are disposed of in the wastewater system.	❒ Low ❒ Medium ❒ High
Water conservation	Only water-conserving fixtures and practices are used. Drips and leaks are fixed immediately.	Some water-conserving steps are taken (such as using low-flow shower heads or fully loading washing machines and dishwashers).	Standard high-volume bathroom fixtures are used (toilets, showers). No effort is made to conserve water. Leaks are not repaired.	❒ Low ❒ Medium ❒ High
Water usage	Laundry and other major water uses are spread out over the week.		Several water-using appliances and fixtures are in use in a short period of time.	❒ Low ❒ High

Go back over the assessment tables to make sure that you recorded all the high and medium risks you identified in the action checklist on the following page. For each medium and high risk uncovered, write down the improvements you plan to make. Use recommendations from this chapter and from other resources to decide upon an action you are likely to complete. A target date will keep you on schedule. You don't have to do everything at once, but try to eliminate the most serious risks as soon as you can. Often it helps to tackle the inexpensive actions first.

For More Information

No matter where you live, there are people in agencies such as Cooperative Extension, health departments, and environmental resource departments who can help. Pumpers, contractors, and laboratories are valuable sources of information as well. The National Small Flows Clearinghouse (NSFC) has several publications on septic system design and maintenance, as well as information about alternative systems. Contact them at NSFC, West Virginia University, P.O. Box 6064, Morgantown, WV 26506-6064, or call (800) 624-8301 to request their catalog. Some of the publications available from NSFC are:

- *Your Septic System: A Reference Guide for Homeowners*, WWBRPE17. This brochure describes a conventional septic system and how it should be cared for to achieve optimal results.

- *The Care and Feeding of Your Septic Tank System*, WWBRPE18. This brochure describes septic tanks and drainfields and provides guidelines to prolong their usefulness.

- *So…Now You Own a Septic Tank*, WWBRPE20. This document describes how a septic tank system works and how to keep it functioning properly.

- *Preventing Pollution Through Efficient Water Us* WWBRPE26. This brochure describes efficient w ter use and its role in preventing pollution.

▶ ACTION CHECKLIST ◀
Household Wastewater:
Septic Systems and Other Treatment Methods

Write all high and medium risks below.	What can you do to reduce the risk?	Set a target date for action.
Sample: Low area over drainfield is always wet.	Have drainfield inspected for blockages, and clean as needed. Divert surface runoff.	One week from today: May 2

- *Homeowner's Septic Tank System Guide and Record Keeping Folder,* WWBLPE30. The National Onsite Wastewater Recycling Association developed this folder to provide septic system owners with simple operation and maintenance guidelines to ensure their system will work properly.

Water testing
Contact your local health department, Cooperative Extension staff, or private testing laboratories.

Groundwater and geology
Contact the office of your state or U.S. Geological Survey, or your local soil and water conservation district.

Drinking water quality standards

Call the U.S. Environmental Protection Agency's Safe Drinking Water Hotline toll-free at (800) 426-4791. The hotline is open from 8:30 A.M. to 5:00 P.M., eastern standard time. Or contact the agency that sets water quality standards in your state (often the department of health).

Water conservation

Many local water utilities have booklets of water conservation tips available. Publications are also available from the American Water Works Association; call (303) 794-7711 for more information. The U.S. Environmental Protection Agency has publications as well, such as document number EPA/841/B-95/002, *Cleaner Water Through Conservation;* to order a copy, contact the National Center for Environmental Publications and Information, P.O. Box 42419, Cincinnati, OH 45242-2419.

*Home*A*Syst* Helps Ensure Your Safety

This *Home*A*Syst* handbook covers a variety of topics to help homeowners examine and address their most important environmental concerns. See the complete list of chapters in the table of contents at the beginning of this handbook. For more information about topics covered in *Home*A*Syst,* or for information about laws and regulations specific to your area, contact your nearest Cooperative Extension office.

Contact the National Farm*A*Syst/Home*A*Syst Office at: B142 Steenbock Library, 550 Babcock Drive, Madison, WI 53706-1293; phone: (608) 262-0024; e-mail: <HOMEASYST@MACC.WISC.EDU>.

This chapter was written by Barbara Kneen Avery, Extension Associate, College of Human Ecology, Cornell Cooperative Extension.

Chapter 5

MANAGING HAZARDOUS HOUSEHOLD PRODUCTS

*by Elaine Andrews, Environmental Resources Center,
University of Wisconsin Cooperative Extension*

Some commercial products commonly used at home have the potential to harm your health and the environment. This chapter will help you identify potential product hazards and minimize your risks. It covers safe management of products, from purchase to disposal. The chapter is divided into three parts:

1. *Product Selection, Purchase, and Use.* This section discusses:
   - product selection criteria
   - how much of a product to purchase
   - safety precautions for use

2. *Safe Storage.* Topics covered in this section include:
   - child safety considerations
   - containers and spill protection
   - proper ventilation

3. *Product Disposal.* This part reviews what to do with leftovers.

Why should you be concerned?

Some products used around the home contain ingredients that can pose threats to your health or the environment if not handled properly (figure 5.1). Vapors from paint thinner and other solvents can be hazardous to breathe. Products such as motor oil or pesticides—if disposed of on the ground—may contribute to the pollution of your drinking water or a nearby stream.

For each chemical or product, there are many questions to consider. Which product best meets your needs? Are there safer alternatives? Is it dangerous to children? What is the best way to store it? How can you use it safely? How do you dispose of leftovers?

This chapter will help you make choices that will reduce risks to your family and your watershed. Remember that you are responsible for the safe use, reuse, or disposal of any products in and around your home. It's up to you to understand how to make a good decision.

Figure 5.1 Some household products contain ingredients that can threaten your health or the environment if not handled properly.

What does the word hazardous mean?

A thing or situation is hazardous if it has the potential to cause harm. For example, a child's rollerskate left on a stair is hazardous.

Household products are hazardous if they include ingredients that, when improperly managed, pose dangers to human health or the environment (see sidebar at right). Not every product in a category of products is hazardous — for example, some paints and strippers are less hazardous than others. To be safe, learn how to properly use, store, and dispose of products.

It is also important to know the difference between hazards to human health and hazards to the environment. These are explained below.

Hazards to human health

Health problems can be caused by chemicals in some of the products in your home *if product warnings and directions for proper use are not heeded.* Health effects can range from minor problems, such as irritated skin or watery eyes, to more serious problems, such as burns, poisoning, or even cancer.

You can be exposed to a product ingredient by (1) ingestion, including accidental ingestion by drinking, eating, or smoking when a substance is on your hands; (2) breathing dust or fumes (inhalation); or (3) contact with skin or eyes (figure 5.2). The potential for harm from exposure to a hazardous product depends on:

- the type of chemicals in the product
- how much of the chemical you are exposed to
- how frequently you are exposed
- your size, weight, and health

If exposure occurs, some harmful effects appear immediately. Typical symptoms are nausea, skin irritation, burning eyes, dizziness, and headaches. Other effects, such as kidney or lung damage or cancer, take a long time to develop. A person who uses hazardous products frequently — without adequate safety precautions or proper ventilation — may experience these serious health effects.

To avoid accidental exposure…

- Follow the safety precautions recommended on the product label.
- Always work in a well-ventilated area, especially if the product contains a solvent. (Solvent-containing products have the words "Flammable," "Combustible," or "Contains Petroleum Distillates" on the label.)

HOUSEHOLD PRODUCTS THAT COULD BE HAZARDOUS IF IMPROPERLY MANAGED *

Building supplies — sealants, some adhesives, wood preservatives

Vehicle-related products — antifreeze, oil, cleaning solvents, lead-acid batteries, gasoline

Home maintenance products — oil-based paints, mineral spirits, products that can remove difficult greases or adhesives, paint stripper

Hobby and recreational supplies — photo developer chemicals, marine paints, electronic equipment cleaners, swimming pool chemicals

Pesticides — herbicides, insecticides, rodent poison, yard insect foggers, chemical strips, fungicides, aquacides

* See the chart on pages 58–60 for a more detailed listing of products.

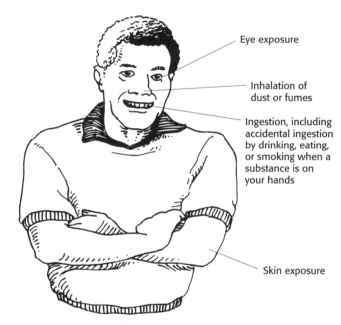

Eye exposure

Inhalation of dust or fumes

Ingestion, including accidental ingestion by drinking, eating, or smoking when a substance is on your hands

Skin exposure

Figure 5.2 You can be exposed to a product ingredient by ingestion, inhalation, and contact with skin or eyes.

- Wear protective clothing such as gloves and goggles when the product label recommends it.
- Remember that label precautions are there for a purpose — to ensure your safety while using the product.

Hazards to the environment

How we manage products used on or near our property can affect the environment. Ingredients in some household products can be hazardous to plants and animals in natural environments. Pesticides or motor oil washing into a stream, for example, can harm fish. Human health can also be threatened if our food, water, or air becomes contaminated through improper use or disposal of a household product. Other chapters in this guide detail management practices for specific categories of contaminants; see the table of contents at the beginning of this book.

Once released, some chemicals can be integrated into the environment without any harmful effects. Others persist and have many different effects. Some chemicals can become integrated into living systems and be passed from one organism to another. If enough of a toxic chemical accumulates, it could harm an organism's ability to reproduce, damage its nervous system, or impair the function of its liver or kidneys.

Most chemicals likely to cause environmental problems are regulated by federal law. But because it is difficult to keep track of the small quantities used by homeowners, everyone needs to do their part to minimize the impact of use and disposal. Some cleanup or disposal practices may not seem like they could lead to trouble, but even old habits should be examined for potential risks.

To protect the environment...
- Avoid...
  - dumping oils, paints, pesticides, or any other household chemicals on the ground, on roads, or down storm sewers
  - dumping products in a wetland, stream, or any other body of water
  - washing chemicals off the driveway with a hose
  - pouring pesticides or non-water-soluble chemicals into a drain that leads to a septic tank
  - spraying pesticides on a windy day
  - burning containers in a barrel or outdoor fire
- Use up a product according to label directions.
- Share any leftovers with a neighbor or local organization.
- Find out if a product can be recycled and where to recycle it in your community.
- Find out if your community has a hazardous waste collection program. Use the community program to dispose of any leftover products listed in the chart on pages 58–60 at the end of this chapter.

PART 1 — Product Selection, Purchase, and Use

Your choice of products is the first step. By carefully selecting the product for the job needed, you can con-

trol the degree of "hazard" you bring to your home or property. At the end of part 1, fill out the assessment table to evaluate your risks regarding product choice and use. The information below will help you answer the questions in the assessment.

How can you tell which products are hazardous?
It is often difficult to find out what is hazardous and to whom and how something is a hazard. It pays to learn as much as you can about a household product and its potential hazards before purchasing the product. Labels contain important information and often tell if a product could be hazardous. Health problems can be avoided by carefully following directions for use and safety.

Remember, *absence* of a warning on a product label does not necessarily mean that the product is safe. Old products or products not designed for household use may not provide consumer information on the label. When using any chemical product, use it with care and caution.

In addition to product labels, up-to-date publications and advice from experts are also good sources of information. Ask questions, and look for helpful ideas from health agency employees, Cooperative Extension staff, articles, and books. See pages 58–60 at the end of this chapter for a listing of products likely to include ingredients of concern.

What can product labels tell us?
Information on the product label can help you decide whether the product is right for the job and if it can be used safely in your situation. Before you purchase or use a product, take the time to read the label, even though the print is often tiny (figure 5.3 on the following page). Labels provide details about how to safely use, store, and dispose of a product. First-aid instructions are provided when needed.

Household consumer products that are hazardous or contain hazardous substances are required to have human safety information, or warning labels. Pesticide labels are also required to provide detailed information on use, storage, and disposal. As you read this section, take a look at the labels on some of the products in your home.

The *signal words* — CAUTION, WARNING, and DANGER — draw your attention to important human safety information. However, they can mean different things, depending on the product. Labels on pesticides provide information about the poison level of the pesticide. On household products, they describe immediate health effects resulting from improper use. The signal word DANGER is required on any product that is extremely flammable, corrosive, or toxic. Products labeled DANGER, FLAMMABLE, POISON, VAPOR HARMFUL, or FATAL IF SWALLOWED may have ingredients that could cause environmental damage as well as health problems if used, stored, or disposed of improperly.

Beware of terms on labels that are vague and possibly misleading. The Federal Trade Commission has provided manufacturers with guidelines about vague environmental terms such as "ozone safe" or "environmentally friendly," but the use of such terms is not regulated on any products except pesticides.

Figure 5.3 Product labels provide details about how to safely use, store, and dispose of a product.

If you need more information about a product than is provided by the label, you may want to request a Material Safety Data Sheet (MSDS) from the manufacturer, or consult a Poison Control Center (see sidebar below right). Most manufacturers provide a phone number on their product label and are willing to answer questions by phone.

Can an alternative product do the job?

When choosing from among several brands of the same kind of product — for example, paint strippers or degreasers — read the labels to learn which product will meet your needs most safely. If you don't check first, you might buy a hazardous product such as a solvent-based cleaner when a detergent-based cleaner is available or a common alternative like kitchen cleanser will work. Manufacturers are aware of consumer safety issues, and many offer a range of products. Some alternatives are suggested in the sidebar on the following page. For more help in deciding which products to buy, check the resources listed on page 56 at the end of this chapter.

In an effort to reduce risk from hazardous chemicals, many organizations have distributed information about making mix-at-home cleaners using readily available ingredients. Be advised, however, that your homemade product may *not* be a safer alternative. If you choose to make your own household products, be sure to consider these precautions:

- Use only one ingredient at a time. Never mix ingredients or products. Be sure to rinse the surface between products used on one place.

- Always test any cleaner on a small area before applying it to the whole surface.

- Do not use food products for cleaning (such as vegetable oil or milk). Food products may spoil or support growth of bacteria or mold on the surface being cleaned.

- Use clean containers when storing homemade products, and clearly label the container with the contents and date. Never store homemade products in old containers from commercial products.

Do you buy only what you need?

If you buy more than you need, household products will accumulate and create storage problems. If unused for long periods, product containers may become

---

IN CASE OF EMERGENCY

Whether you are using a cleaning product or a pesticide, don't rely *only* on the label for information on health emergencies or environmental dangers. The information may be incomplete or incorrect. **Poison Control Centers** — whose resources feature a national computer data network — can provide *emergency* health information about a product. Look up your local or state number, write it here:

_____

and keep the number close to your phone. For information about spills of hazardous products, contact your state natural resources or agriculture agency, or the National Response Center at (800) 424-8802.

damaged and leak, and products may change chemically and not be effective when you finally try to use them. Some products such as pesticides may have been restricted or banned since they were purchased. If that occurs, safe and legal disposal becomes much more difficult. Avoid these problems by purchasing and using only what you need.

<table>
<tr><td colspan="2">

LOOKING FOR AN ALTERNATIVE?

Adhesives — Use a water-based or latex adhesive.

Batteries—Choose rechargeable batteries (removable, so they can be recycled) and mercury-free batteries when possible.

Cleaners—Choose soap- or detergent-based cleaners when possible. Avoid non-water-soluble and corrosive cleaners when others offer an effective substitute.

Household pesticides—Look for ways to reduce your need for these products through appropriate cleaning and maintenance habits.

Floor and wood-finish strippers—Use a detergent or water-based stripper.

Paint stripper—Use sandpaper, a scraper, or heat gun for small jobs.

Wood preservative—Use a water-sealing coating.

Several of the above suggestions were provided by the Minnesota Pollution Control Agency.

</td></tr>
</table>

Assessment 1 — Product selection, purchase, and use

The risk categories and recommendations found in the assessment table below and others that follow apply to hazardous products in general. For some products, there will be management options that are not covered. If you are not sure what to do, don't take chances. Find out what is safe.

Use the table to rate your risks related to the selection, purchase, and use of household products. (Parts 2 and 3 in this chapter cover storage and disposal.) For each question, indicate your risk level in the right-hand column. Some choices may not be exactly like your situation, so choose the response that best fits. Refer to part 1 above if you need more information to complete this table.

Responding to risks

Your goal is to lower your health risks and reduce potential harm to the environment. Turn to the action checklist on page 57 to record the medium- and high-risk practices you identified. Use the recommendations above to help you plan actions to reduce your risks.

▶ **ASSESSMENT 1 — Product Selection, Purchase, and Use**

	LOW RISK	MEDIUM RISK	HIGH RISK	YOUR RISK
Product selection	I always read labels; understand signal words; and respect the health or environmental hazards labels describe. I choose the least hazardous product needed for the job.	I don't read labels or don't understand what they mean, but I use a "common sense" approach to safety.	I never read labels. I purchase products without considering what the product is made of or how it will be used.	❑ Low ❑ Medium ❑ High
Quantities purchased	I buy only what is needed for a specific job. I use up most of the product within a few months after purchase or give excess away to someone else.	I buy excess product, but provide safe and accessible storage.	I buy more than is needed, then purchase additional product without checking on current supplies.	❑ Low ❑ Medium ❑ High
Safety precautions*	I follow label instructions and take recommended precautions against exposure (such as providing good ventilation and wearing safety goggles and gloves). I never mix products.	I occasionally read label instructions. I take some precautions. I occasionally mix products for specific cleaning tasks, but I always check safety precautions first.	I never follow label instructions and take no precautions — even when recommended. If one product doesn't work, I add in another without checking safety precautions.	❑ Low ❑ Medium ❑ High

* Safe disposal is also part of safety precautions. See part 3, "Product Disposal," for tips.

PART 2 — Safe Storage

Leftover or used chemicals such as strippers, paint, waste oil, used antifreeze, and solvents may need to be stored until their next use or disposal (figure 5.4). How you store household products can determine how much risk may be present. Use the information below to help you fill out the assessment table at the end of this section.

Are your storage locations and containers really safe?

When storing household products, the primary concerns are child safety (figure 5.5), indoor air quality, and prevention of damage to household equipment or the environment. If you can smell a household product while it is in storage, the product lid may be loose or ventilation may be inadequate to protect your health.

WHEN YOU STORE HOUSEHOLD PRODUCTS, DO YOU:

- Keep them out of the reach of children and pets, preferably in a locked, secure area?

- Store them in their original containers?

- Clearly label and date any alternative containers?

- Keep containers tightly sealed and dry?

- Store products at least 150 feet from a well or waterway?

- Keep products in a well-ventilated area and away from sources of ignition?

- Store batteries and flammable chemicals in an area shaded from direct sunlight?

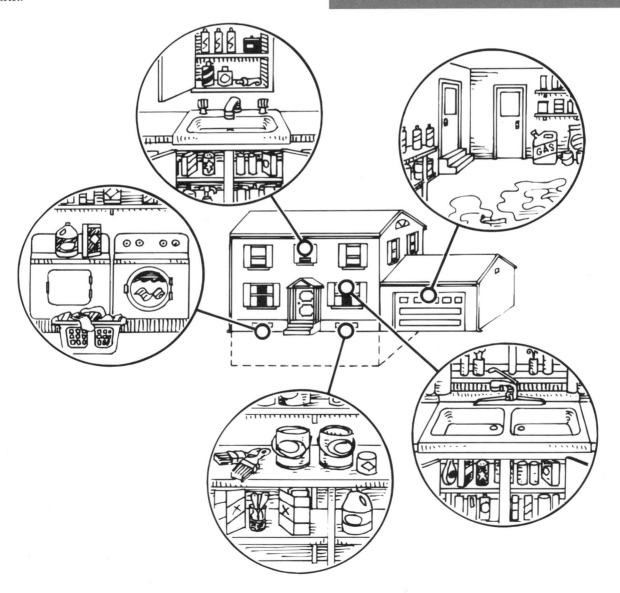

Figure 5.4 Hazardous products may be stored throughout a household.

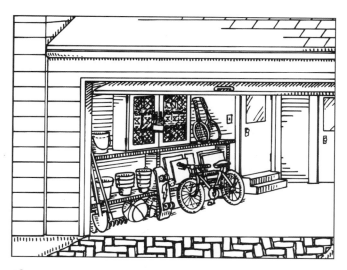

Figure 5.5 Hazardous products should be stored in a locked cabinet or other location inaccessible to children.

Be sure to separate corrosives like acids or lye from each other and other hazardous products to prevent dangerous chemical reactions. Reactions occur when corrosives leak from their containers and drip or flow to other products. Corrosive materials are often stored where equipment and appliances are located; be aware that they can corrode air conditioning and heating systems, hot water heaters, and other equipment or appliances. Routinely check areas where you store household products (under the kitchen sink, in the basement or garage) to make sure that containers are closed tightly and not leaking, and that the sides of containers are not bulging.

Assessment 2 — Safe storage

Use the table below to rate your risks related to product storage. For each question, indicate your risk level in the right-hand column. Some choices may not be exactly like your situation, so choose the response that best fits. Refer to part 2 above if you need more information to complete this table. See part 1 for choices about product selection and part 3 for choices about disposal.

Responding to risks

Your goal is to lower your health risks and reduce potential harm to the environment. Turn to the action checklist on page 57 to record the medium- and high-risk practices you identified. Use the recommendations above to help you plan actions to reduce your risks.

PART 3 — Product Disposal

Unless a product is used up, you will have to dispose of it. For some products that are especially hazardous — like pesticides — even the product *container* will have to be disposed of properly. Part 3 provides tips for disposal of certain hazardous product categories, but readers are referred to the disposal guides listed on page 56 at the end of this chapter for detailed management recommendations.

▶ ASSESSMENT 2 — Safe Storage

	LOW RISK	MEDIUM RISK	HIGH RISK	YOUR RISK
Child safety	I store hazardous products in a locked cabinet or other location inaccessible to children.	I keep products out of the direct reach of children (on a high shelf, for example) but still accessible.	My products are easily accessible to children (for example, in an unlocked cabinet on the lower shelf).	❏ Low ❏ Medium ❏ High
Containers, storage location, and spill protection	I store leftovers in their original containers, properly sealed. Products are stored by type. My home environment is protected against leaks or spills.	I store original containers in a disorganized way. I don't provide protection against leaks or spills.	I transfer leftovers to other containers such as used milk jugs or glass jars. I store leftovers without caps or lids. I don't provide protection against leaks or spills.	❏ Low ❏ Medium ❏ High
Ventilation	I store volatile products (like solvents and petroleum-based fluids) in places with good ventilation.	I don't pay attention to storage location, but each container is in good shape and tightly sealed.	I store products in areas with poor ventilation such as basements, closets, or crawl spaces. Containers are damaged or left open.	❏ Low ❏ Medium ❏ High

What is the best way to dispose of leftover hazardous products?

Disposal should be your last option because it is wasteful and, if not done properly, can be unsafe for you and the environment. You can avoid the disposal dilemma by buying and using only what you need, using up your leftovers, or recycling. By giving leftover products to a neighbor or local organization who can use them, you can turn a potential waste problem into a cost-saving opportunity.

Some communities sponsor swap programs to encourage sharing, and options for recycling are increasing. Used motor oil and antifreeze, for example, are accepted in many communities and automobile repair shops for recycling (figure 5.6). Some pesticide containers may be returned to where they were purchased for safe disposal.

Some cities and communities sponsor either occasional or permanent household hazardous waste collection programs. Because only certain hazardous products may be accepted, contact the program to learn exactly what materials are accepted. If your community does not sponsor such a program, contact local sanitation officials for disposal advice.

Household quantities of some products can be safely sent to a landfill. For example, leftover paint—if local regulations permit—can be evaporated in its can. When dry, the can with its hardened contents can be discarded in household garbage.

Paint and pesticides merit special attention

We all buy too much paint. Municipalities that collect leftover hazardous household products report that paints make up about half of the material that people bring and thus are a costly (but avoidable) disposal expense. The best practice is to avoid leftovers by calculating how much paint you'll need before you buy. Salespeople at paint stores can help you with these calculations.

Most leftover paint can be safely managed by sharing it with neighbors or organizations. However, leftover lead-based paints or exterior paints containing mercury or pesticides should be treated as hazardous waste.

We don't pay enough attention to how we manage pesticides. A 1992 U.S. Environmental Protection Agency study of pesticide use in homes and gardens provided disturbing information about how pesticides are used, stored, and thrown away. Household practices showed that people fail to recognize the danger that pesticides can pose to child safety, human health, or the environment when managed improperly.

Before you choose a pesticide, be sure that you have exhausted other options for managing the pest, weed, or fungus problem (see suggestions in the sidebar below). If you do need to use a pesticide, read label information carefully before purchasing a product. Buy only what you need.

Pay attention to use and disposal recommendations described on labels. Before disposal, use up the product if possible. Rinse empty containers of liquid pesticides. Use the rinse water as part of your yard and garden management. Chapter 7 provides additional advice for managing yard and garden pesticides.

Figure 5.6 Used motor oil and antifreeze are accepted in many communities for recycling.

> ### REDUCE YOUR NEED FOR PESTICIDES IN THE HOME
>
> - Maintain regular cleaning habits, especially in the kitchen area.
> - Caulk cracks and other openings to the outside.
> - Keep screens repaired.
> - Keep houseplants healthy by providing appropriate care.

Is dumping or burning a safe alternative?

It is *never* appropriate to dump or burn hazardous products on your property, particularly near wells or water sources. Nor should products be poured down storm sewers. Water-soluble cleaning products may be safely disposed down the drain if you flush the drain with plenty of water.

Septic system owners need to be especially careful, however. With septic systems, the rule of thumb is moderation. Don't dump large amounts of *anything* into the septic system. Septic systems are not designed to treat chemicals. If the product is specifically designed to be used in the home with water, then moderate use will not harm the system.

Burning hazardous wastes in a barrel or stove is never an alternative — and it's illegal in many states. Burning may release toxic gases and produce hazardous ash.

Assessment 3 — Product disposal

General recommendations for disposal are provided in the table below. Check the waste category in the left column and see if any of your disposal practices present risks to human health or the environment. (See the chart beginning on page 58 — Hazardous Product Examples and Inventory — for specific products affected by these recommendations.)

Responding to risks

Your goal is to lower your risks. Turn to the action checklist on page 57 to record the medium- and high-risk practices you identified. Use the recommendations above to help you plan actions to reduce your risks.

▶ ASSESSMENT 3 — Product Disposal

WASTE CATEGORY*	LOW RISK	MEDIUM RISK	HIGH RISK	YOUR RISK
Household trash Trash containing plastics or empty containers of hazardous ingredients.	I rinse empty yard and garden pesticide containers and include rinse water in yard and garden management. I dispose of ash, mixed trash, and empty product containers at the community landfill. I do not burn trash.	I dispose of ash from mixed trash, leftover pesticides, and solvents on my property, but away from my well or waterway. I burn hazardous containers.	I always dispose of ash from mixed trash, leftover pesticides, and solvents near a well or waterway. I burn hazardous containers near people or animals.	❏ Low ❏ Medium ❏ High
Strong acids and bases Found in hobby and recreation products, concentrated building cleaners, and building repair products.	I share any leftover products. I dilute strong acids and bases and pour them down a drain that connects to a sewage treatment facility.	I pour strong acids and cleaners down the drain without first diluting them with water. I send leftovers to a landfill (with proper protection for garbage haulers and employees).	I pour strong acids and cleaners directly into a storm sewer or waterway or on a paved slope leading to a waterway.	❏ Low ❏ Medium ❏ High
Antifreeze, waste motor oil	I recycle antifreeze and waste motor oil by taking them to properly qualified dumping stations.	I pour my used antifreeze into a septic system or municipal treatment system.	I dump used antifreeze and waste oil always in the same place, near a well or waterway. I dump these materials directly into a waterway.	❏ Low ❏ Medium ❏ High
Batteries May contain mercury, cadmium, or lead.	I recycle batteries or take them to a hazardous waste disposal program.	I dispose of batteries in a community landfill.	I always dump batteries near a well or waterway.	❏ Low ❏ Medium ❏ High

* Refer to the inventory chart on pages 58–60 for examples of some categories.

continued on next page ▶

WASTE CATEGORY*	LOW RISK	MEDIUM RISK	HIGH RISK	YOUR RISK
Bottled gas	I recycle bottled gas containers.	I store containers that may still contain some gas.	I put containers in my trash or leave them lying around.	❐ Low ❐ Medium ❐ High
Cleaning and repair products containing hazardous solvents (non-water-soluble) and paint	I share leftovers when possible. I take leftover products containing mercury, pesticides, or hazardous solvents to a hazardous waste disposal program.	I dispose of leftover products in a community landfill.	I always dump leftover products. I dump leftovers near a well or waterway. I dump all my leftovers directly into a waterway. (NOTE: This is illegal!)	❐ Low ❐ Medium ❐ High
Fluorescent bulbs Contain mercury.	I recycle burned-out fluorescent bulbs or lamps.	I put my burned-out bulbs in the trash.	I leave my burned-out bulbs at a dump.	❐ Low ❐ Medium ❐ High
Pesticides See chapter 7, "Yard and Garden Care" (page 69), for more information.	I use preventive actions to control pests, indoors and outdoors. I explore options for nonchemical pest controls. I properly choose, store, handle, apply, and dispose of chemical pest controls.	When solving pest problems, I do not practice much prevention or explore nonchemical options.	I DO NOT handle pesticides as directed on the label.	❐ Low ❐ Medium ❐ High

* Refer to the inventory chart on pages 58–60 for examples of some categories.

ACTION CHECKLIST

When you finish the assessments, go back over them to make sure you have recorded all medium and high risks in the checklist. For each risk you identified, write down the improvements you plan to make. Use recommendations from this chapter and other resources (see "For More Information" below). Pick a target date to keep you on schedule for making changes. You don't have to do everything at once, but try to eliminate the most serious risks as soon as you can. Often it helps to start with inexpensive actions first.

For More Information

Managing hazardous household products

Contact your local, county, or state government. No matter where you live, there are government and agency personnel who can help.

Managing pesticides

See chapter 7, "Yard and Garden Care," which begins on page 69. For detailed guidance on pesticide management, see *Guides to Pollution Prevention: Non-Agri-*

cultural Pesticide Users, United States Environmental Protection Agency, 1993, document EPA/625/R-93/009. This 58-page guide, which includes nine worksheets, is available from the National Center for Environmental Publications and Information, P.O. Box 42419, Cincinnati, OH 45242-2419; fax (513) 489-8695.

Disposal

The Water Environment Federation's (WEF) waste disposal guide provides disposal recommendations for many kinds of products. You may be able to get one from your local sewage treatment facility or contact WEF, Public Information Department, 601 Wythe Street, Alexandria, VA 22314-1994; phone (800) 666-0206 or (703) 684-2452.

Other guides are available from the Environmental Hazards Management Institute (EHMI). For more information, write to them at 10 Newmarket Road, Durham, NH 03824; phone (800) 558-EHMI; fax (603) 868-1547; or e-mail <EHMIORG@AOL.COM>. Your local Cooperative Extension office may have similar guides.

► ACTION CHECKLIST ◄
Managing Hazardous Household Products

Write all high and medium risks below.	What can you do to reduce the risk?	Set a target date for action.
Sample: Cabinet with antifreeze and paint stripper is not child-proof.	Buy a lock and install it on cabinet.	One week from today: November 28

*Home*A*Syst* Helps Ensure Your Safety

This *Home*A*Syst* handbook covers a variety of topics to help homeowners examine and address their most important environmental concerns. See the complete list of chapters in the table of contents at the beginning of this handbook. For more information about topics covered in *Home*A*Syst*, or for information about laws and regulations specific to your area, contact your nearest Cooperative Extension office.

Contact the National Farm*A*Syst/Home*A*Syst Office at: B142 Steenbock Library, 550 Babcock Drive, Madison, WI 53706-1293; phone: (608) 262-0024; e-mail: <HOMEASYST@MACC.WISC.EDU>.

This chapter was written by Elaine Andrews, Environmental Education Specialist, Environmental Resources Center, University of Wisconsin Cooperative Extension. Information on accidental exposure to hazardous products was adapted from a fact sheet produced by the Minnesota Pollution Control Agency.

Hazardous Product Examples and Inventory

Check for hazardous products stored in your home. Use the list below to plan ways to improve your use, storage, and/or disposal of these products. If you are unsure about disposal, contact your local Cooperative Extension office or state environmental protection agency.

Category/product	Is it properly stored?	Is information about proper disposal needed?	Are there special precautions to keep in mind?
HOUSEHOLD TRASH			
Ash/sludge from burned home or garage trash (*Note:* Burning trash is illegal in many states!)			
Fluorescent bulbs/lamps (contain mercury)			
Waste motor oil			
Plastic wraps and containers (only hazardous when burned)			
Pesticide or solvent containers			
Empty containers from other product categories listed below			
CLOTHING AND FABRIC CARE PRODUCTS			
Mothballs			
Dry-cleaning fluids			
Spot removers (solvent-based)			
Shoe/leather polishes			
HOBBY AND RECREATION PRODUCTS			
Artist paints and solvents			
Charcoal lighter fluid			
Strong acids/bases*			
Bottled gas			
Household batteries (may contain mercury or cadmium)			
BUILDING/WOOD CLEANERS AND REPAIR PRODUCTS			
Building and wood cleaners with organic solvent ingredients:			
• Wood polishes			
• Products for wood floor and panel cleaning			

* See note on page 60.

continued on next page ▶

Home*A*Syst: An Environmental Risk-Assessment Guide for the Home

Category/product	Is it properly stored?	Is information about proper disposal needed?	Are there special precautions to keep in mind?
BUILDING/WOOD CLEANERS AND REPAIR PRODUCTS (continued)			
Building and equipment maintenance products:			
• Strong acids, bases*			
• Lead-based paint (see chapter 6, "Lead In and Around the Home," for more information)			
• Oil/alkyd paints and primers			
• Marine and exterior paints containing mercury and/or pesticides			
• Aerosol paint products			
• Stains and finishes			
• Roof coatings and sealants			
• Rust removers			
• Silicon lubricants			
• Other lubricants			
• Adhesive removers			
• Paint and finish preparation products			
• Adhesives such as glues and caulk			
• Wood-preserving products			
• Products for brush or spray gun cleaning			
• Water repellents for wood and cement			
• Solvents, as those used in degreasers and paint thinners, stains, and varnishes			
PESTICIDES			
Pesticides labeled "restrictive-use"			
General-use pesticides			
Old pesticides			
Unwanted pesticides			

* See note on page 60.

continued on next page ▶

Category/product	Is it properly stored?	Is information about proper disposal needed?	Are there special precautions to keep in mind?
VEHICLE MAINTENANCE CHEMICALS			
Vehicle maintenance products such as antifreeze, oil and grease, and transmission fluid			
Solvents for oil and grease removal and disposal			
Engine and parts cleaners such as carburetor and brake cleaner			
Paints and paint preparation products			
Lead acid batteries			
Battery terminal protector			
Tire cleaners			
Rust removers			
Ignition wire dryer			
Gasket removers			
Aerosol paint and primer products			
Brake quieter			
Brush and spray gun cleaners			

NOTE: You can identify strong acids or bases in the product you are using by noting:

- if the hazard warning label recommends that the user wear skin protection or avoid breathing the vapors or aerosol mists
- if the product was intended for commercial use (industrial-strength cleaner, for example)
- if the product was intended to manage difficult stains or dirt on hard surfaces (for example, rust or lime remover)

Now that you have completed this inventory, you are more familiar with hazardous products found in your home. Review the inventory once again and consider the following:

- Do I need all of these products in my home?
- Are there less hazardous alternatives I can use?
- Do I have as much information as I need to make good use, storage, and disposal decisions?

Chapter 6

by Karen Filchak, University of Connecticut
Cooperative Extension

LEAD IN AND AROUND THE HOME: Identifying and Managing Its Sources

This chapter addresses sources of lead in and around the home and explains the health hazards associated with exposure to lead. The chapter is divided into three parts:

1. *Identifying Lead Sources Inside the Home*
   - Lead-based paint in or on pre-1978 homes
   - Lead in drinking water from contact with lead pipes, lead-based solder, or other plumbing sources

2. *Identifying Lead Sources Outside the Home*
   - Leaded exterior paint
   - Automobile exhaust
   - Industry

3. *Health Effects of Lead on Children*
   - Avenues of exposure
   - Effects and symptoms of poisoning

Completing this chapter will help you identify and evaluate lead-related risks to your family's health. Tips are given for reducing those risks.

Why should you be concerned?

Lead is a soft metal that has been used in ammunition, ceramics, printer's ink, solder, paint, coins, leaded crystal, and water pipes; as a gasoline additive; and for many other purposes. Lead is dangerous because it is so widely used and lasts forever in the environment. It never breaks down into a harmless substance. You can take steps to reduce your exposure to lead, but you cannot completely avoid it. Reducing exposure is especially important for children.

Lead poisoning is a serious but preventable health problem. Many public health experts consider it the number one environmental health problem in the United States. Many homes have one or more sources of lead. An estimated one in nine American children

has an elevated blood-lead level, and the chief suspect is lead-based paint from older homes. Families can also be exposed to lead from their drinking water and other sources.

Lead, depending upon the level, can have wide-ranging effects in humans. Even very low lead levels in children can slow mental development and cause learning and behavioral problems. Lead can also cause high blood pressure in adults. Higher levels may cause damage to the nervous system and the reproductive system. Sadly, the effects of lead poisoning are frequently irreversible.

Where are the lead sources in and around your home?

The most common sources of lead are lead-based paint, household dust (which can contain lead dust from deteriorating lead-based paint or remodeling), soils contaminated by leaded gasoline exhaust and disintegrating lead-based paint, and drinking water delivered through lead pipes or in contact with lead solder. Over the years, lead has been eliminated by law in residential paint, gasoline, solder, and water pipes. However, many older homes contain lead paint, and even newer homes can contain lead from other sources. Unlike many chemicals, lead does not break down and can remain for long periods in paints, dusts, and soil.

PART 1 — Identifying Lead Sources Inside the Home

Identifying and controlling sources of lead in and around your home is an important responsibility. To determine potential risks from sources inside your home, complete the assessment table at the end of part 1. The information below will help you answer the assessment questions.

When was your home built?

According to the U.S. Department of Housing and Urban Development, 74% of all homes built before 1980 contain potentially dangerous levels of lead paint. Although lead has been banned from house paint since 1978, the majority of U.S. homes were built before then. Homes built before 1950 are very likely to have high lead levels, especially in paint used on windows and exterior surfaces. Levels as high as 25 to 35% lead by weight are common. Some pre-1950 paint was 50% lead.

Does your interior paint contain lead, and what is its condition?

Lead-based paint (LBP) is the most common source of high lead exposure for children. Most exposure, however, comes from contact with contaminated household dust rather than from eating paint chips. As paint ages or as painted surfaces rub against each other, lead-containing dust is created. If your LBP is perfectly intact, then the potential risk of accidental ingestion is greatly reduced. But if lead paint is cracking, chipping, flaking, or being rubbed by contact, then the danger of lead exposure is much higher.

Testing for lead

To find out if your paint contains lead—and if so, how much—have it analyzed by experts who test samples in a laboratory or who examine paint on-site using a portable X-ray fluorescence (XRF) detector. Surface-wipe samples, which are used to test dust for lead contamination, may be taken by professional inspectors and sent to a lab for analysis. Some laboratories may analyze surface-wipe samples collected by the homeowner. Do-it-yourself home test kits are available in stores. They indicate the presence or absence of lead but do not indicate *how much* lead is present. Home test kits may not be reliable for testing surfaces in your home; it is best to have such tests done by a professional. Check with local health officials or state or national lead information resources to find out what testing options are available. (See "For More Information" on page 67.)

If you find lead...

Remodeling or renovating in areas having LBP is especially risky. Scraping, sanding, or burning LBP creates extremely hazardous conditions, and strict precautions need to be taken—especially if children, pregnant women, or pets are present. If possible, homeowners should use the services of a certified lead inspector and lead-abatement contractor. Paint removal, replacement of lead-painted parts (such as windows, door jambs, and moldings), liquid encapsulants (special paint-like products that cover a surface), and removal off-site of leaded surfaces are some of the options for dealing with lead paint. LBP removal by untrained workers who do not use the proper methods and equipment can create a much greater health hazard than just leaving the paint alone.

Is there lead paint on windows and door frames, and what is its condition?

Lead was added to paint to inhibit the growth of mold on the surface of the paint. Thus, paints with higher

---

HOW MUCH LEAD IS IN YOUR PAINT?

Keep good records of any testing so you and future owners can properly manage painted surfaces. Write the results of lead tests here:

Location of paint sample	Amount of lead found (percentage by weight or milligrams/square centimeter)	Date of test

lead levels were used where exposure to moisture is greatest: on windows, doors, and exterior walls. If high-lead LBP is intact, it poses little risk. But if it is chipping or chalking off, or is scraped or sanded during repairs, then the risk of exposure is great (figure 6.1). Lead dust, which is the form most easily ingested, is likely to come from weathering (chalking) paint and especially from surfaces that rub or slide together, such as a window in its frame.

Is your drinking water lead-free?

Although your drinking water is not usually a concentrated lead source like paint or soil, it can still pose risks to your family. Lead can enter your water from several points: lead pipes that bring water to the home, lead pipe connectors, lead-soldered joints in copper plumbing, and lead-containing brass faucets and pump components. In some private wells, underwater pumps with brass fittings can cause elevated lead concentrations in drinking water, especially with new pumps or if the water is soft. Water that is soft or acidic can be corrosive and tends to dissolve lead from pipes and fittings more easily. Home water softeners, though they do have benefits, may increase the amount of lead leached into your drinking water *if* lead is present in your water system.

What can you do to minimize lead in your water?

Water testing will show if lead is present in your water and whether your water is "aggressive" (acidic or soft). Contact a state-certified laboratory or health agency for instructions on how to take a water sample (figure 6.2). If lead levels are greater than 15 parts per billion (ppb), action is recommended.

Figure 6.2 A state-certified laboratory can provide a water sample container and instructions on how to take a water sample.

Figure 6.1 Lead-based paint chips can be easily ingested by children.

HOW ELSE CAN LEAD ENTER THE HOME?

1. **In consumer products.** Lead is present in such products as lead-crystal glassware and leaded wine bottle neck wraps made before 1990. It may also be in some foreign-made products such as toys (which may have leaded paint), miniblinds, chalk, crayons, and food cans (which may be made with lead solder). Although lead is now less common in printing inks, it may be present in food packaging labels and newspaper print.

2. **From the workplace.** Do you work in construction, bridge building, sandblasting, shipbuilding, plumbing, battery manufacturing, auto radiator repair, furniture refinishing, or foundry casting? If so, lead-contaminated dust from your work site can be carried unknowingly into your home on your clothing or skin. Workers exposed to leaded dusts should shower and change clothes before entering their homes.

3. **In hobby and recreation supplies.** If your hobbies include stained glass, furniture refinishing, pottery (using lead glazes), or collecting pewter or lead figurines, you may be exposing yourself and others to lead. Hunters and fishers who use or make lead bullets and lead sinkers also come in contact with lead. Exposure can also occur at indoor firing ranges.

4. **In ethnic medicinals or cosmetics.** Various Hispanic and Asiatic communities utilize mixtures that contain high levels of lead. Some of the stomach preparations are actually quite toxic.

A simple way to reduce lead concentrations is to flush your plumbing system. You must, however, test a sample from flushed water to be sure that it is below the lead level of 15 ppb. If your water system has not been used for more than four hours, flush the system by letting the cold water run for a minute or two before using it for drinking or cooking.

Also, always use cold tap water for cooking and drinking; hot water is more likely to dissolve lead. Never use water with high lead levels (over 15 ppb) to mix infant formula. For severe lead contamination, you may need to install a water treatment device, such as a reverse osmosis system, a distillation system, or an activated carbon filter. Buying bottled water for drinking and cooking may be the easiest and least expensive option for dealing with severe lead contamination (figure 6.3). Be aware, however, that bottled water is not necessarily lead-free; call or write to the company and request a copy of their most recent water test results.

Assessment 1 — Identifying lead sources inside the home

Use the assessment table on the following page to rate your lead-related indoor health risks. For each question, indicate your risk level in the right-hand column. Although some choices may not correspond exactly to your situation, choose the response that best fits. Refer to the information in part 1 if you need help completing the table.

Figure 6.3 Bottled water for drinking and cooking is one option for dealing with lead-contaminated water.

Responding to risks

Your goal is to lower your risks. Turn to the action checklist on page 68 to record the medium- and high-risk situations. Plan actions to help you reduce your risks.

PART 2 — Identifying Lead Sources Outside the Home

Is your family tracking lead into the home?

The soil around your home can be a significant source of lead exposure, and levels tend to be highest where house walls meet the ground (figure 6.4). Lead-contaminated soil is a problem when children play outdoors, when soil is tracked inside the home, and when vegetables are grown in contaminated soil. Soils may be contaminated by flaking, peeling, or chalking lead-based paint that follows the "drip line" of the house.

In high auto traffic areas, leaded gasoline exhaust has been responsible for high levels of lead in soil, with levels highest near major roadways. The shift to unleaded gasoline has reduced this risk, but after years of contamination, lead levels can still be high.

If you live near industrial sources such as incinerators, lead smelters, and battery recyclers, you should be concerned about lead in your soil. Urban residents should consider having their soil tested before planting a vegetable garden.

What can soil tests reveal?

Testing your soil is the only way to detect a lead problem. Many laboratories can provide this testing. Some local health departments or Cooperative Extension offices may also test soil for free or a small fee. If high lead levels are found, there are several steps you can take. Planting grass or covering soil with mulch can keep your family from tracking the soil indoors or breathing soil dust. In some cases, removal and replacement of heavily contaminated topsoil may be recommended.

What level is safe?

Relatively safe background levels in soils range from non-detectable to 200 parts per million (ppm). Soils with lead levels of 500 ppm or more should not be used for growing vegetables unless the top 6 to 8 inches are replaced with non-contaminated topsoil. In undisturbed soil, lead is usually found in the top 2 to 3 inches.

Lead levels in soil within 85 feet of busy roadways are typically 30 to 2,000 ppm higher than natural levels, and some soils have as much as 10,000 ppm. Soils

adjacent to houses with leaded exterior paint may also have lead levels as high as 10,000 ppm. Levels near industrial sources can be dangerously high, especially in areas downwind. Old orchards may also have high lead levels due to lead-containing pesticides applied in the 1940s.

Assessment 2 — Identifying lead sources outside the home

Use the assessment table on the following page to rate your health risks due to lead outdoors. For each question, indicate your risk level in the right-hand column. Although some choices may not correspond exactly to your situation, choose the response that best fits. Refer to the information in part 2 if you need help completing the table.

Responding to risks

Your goal is to lower your risks. Turn to the action checklist on page 68 to record medium- and high-risk situations. Plan actions to help reduce your risks.

Figure 6.4 Chipped paint can cause lead contamination of soil.

▶ ASSESSMENT 1 — Identifying Lead Sources Inside the Home

	LOW RISK	MEDIUM RISK	HIGH RISK	YOUR RISK
Age of home	Built after 1978.	Built between 1950 and 1978.	Built before 1950.	❑ Low ❑ Medium ❑ High
Interior paint	No lead-based paint.	Lead-based paint present but intact.	Defective lead-based paint: it is chipping, peeling, or chalking or recent remodeling has disturbed the paint.	❑ Low ❑ Medium ❑ High
Windows and doors	No lead-based paint, or windows and doors with lead-based paint have been replaced.	Lead-based paint present but intact.	Defective lead-based paint: it is chipping, peeling, or chalking or untrained workers have recently removed the paint.	❑ Low ❑ Medium ❑ High
Water supply	No lead water pipes, leaded solder, or brass fixtures used in plumbing.	Lead present in plumbing, but water has been tested and precautions have been taken.	Lead likely to be present in plumbing, but water has not been tested and no precautions have been taken.	❑ Low ❑ Medium ❑ High
Water acidity or corrosiveness	Hardness is around 80 milligrams/liter. pH = 7.5–8.5	Hardness is 60–80 milligrams/liter. pH = 6–7.5	Hardness is 60 milligrams/liter or less. pH = less than 6	❑ Low ❑ Medium ❑ High

	LOW RISK	MEDIUM RISK	HIGH RISK	YOUR RISK
Lead-based paint (LBP) on exterior of house	No LBP, or LBP is present but intact. There is a lawn or dense landscape plantings around the side of the home.	LBP is weathered or chalking. There is LBP in the soil around the home, but foot traffic is kept away.	LBP is chipping, peeling, or chalking. There is bare soil or foot traffic below painted walls.	❏ Low ❏ Medium ❏ High
Major roadways	No major roadway nearby.		Major roadway within 85 feet.	❏ Low ❏ High
Lead-related industry	No lead-related industry or incinerators in the area.		Lead smelter, battery manufacturer or recycler, or other lead-related industry nearby.	❏ Low ❏ High

PART 3 — Health Effects of Lead on Children

If children live in or visit your home, have they been tested for lead?

Children six years old and younger are much more likely to be affected by lead than adults. Because they naturally engage in hand-to-mouth activities, they are more likely to accidentally ingest lead. Children are at greatest risk from lead because their bodies are developing, and they absorb up to 50% of the lead they ingest. Adults absorb only about 10%.

Most children with elevated blood-lead levels do not show visible symptoms. A blood test is the only way to detect the problem (figure 6.5). The lowest levels of lead poisoning have no outward symptoms but can damage the brain. At higher levels of poisoning, symptoms may include tiredness, a short attention span, restlessness, poor appetite, constipation, headache, sudden behavior change, vomiting, and hearing loss. Many of these symptoms may be mistaken for other illnesses.

Since lead is widespread in our environment, it is almost impossible to have a zero level in the blood. Lead levels are measured in micrograms per deciliter ($\mu g/dL$) of blood. Levels of 10 $\mu g/dL$ or higher are considered elevated in children and are likely to cause negative effects.

Assessment 3 — Health effects of lead in children

Use the table on the following page to rate your children's health risks due to lead. Indicate the risk level in the right-hand column. Refer to the information above if you need help completing the table.

Responding to risks

Your goal is to lower your risks. Turn to the action checklist on page 68 to record the medium- and high-risk situations you identified. Plan actions to help reduce your risks.

Figure 6.5 A blood test is the only way to detect elevated blood lead levels in children.

	LOW RISK	MEDIUM RISK	HIGH RISK	YOUR RISK
Blood test results in children	Blood-lead level is under 10 µg/dL.	Blood-lead level is 10–19 µg/dL.	Blood-lead level is 20 µg/dL or higher.	❏ Low ❏ Medium ❏ High

ACTION CHECKLIST

Go over the three assessment tables to make sure you have recorded all of your high and medium risks in the action checklist on the following page. Next, write the actions or improvements you plan to make. Use the information provided in this chapter to help pick an action you are likely to complete. Write down a date for carrying out your plan. You don't have to do everything at once, but try to eliminate the most serious risks as soon as you can. Often it helps to tackle the inexpensive actions first.

For More Information

Blood tests
Contact your family physician or pediatrician or public health clinics.

Testing of paint samples and drinking water
Contact your local health department or private testing laboratories.

Educational information for parents and others
Contact the nearest Cooperative Extension office.

National Lead Information Center
To order a packet of materials about lead, including information specific to your state and locality, call the center toll-free at (800) LEAD-FYI. For personal assistance on a lead-related question, call (800) 424-LEAD.

Your state's department of public health
There may be an office in your state that deals with lead-related health issues. They can offer advice and possibly financial assistance for testing and abatement.

Poison control centers
Write your state's toll-free number here:

_____

and keep it by your phone.

Publications
"Preventing Lead Poisoning in Young Children." October 1991. Centers for Disease Control (CDC), U.S. Department of Health and Human Services. Contact the CDC at 4770 Buford Highway, Atlanta, GA 30341-3724; phone (770) 488-7330.

"Lead in Your Drinking Water: Actions You Can Take to Reduce Lead in Drinking Water." Publication EPA/810/F93/001. June 1993. U.S. Environmental Protection Agency fact sheet. Available from the National Center for Environmental Publications and Information, P.O. Box 42419, Cincinnati, OH 45242-2419; fax (513) 489-8695.

"Reducing Lead Hazards When Remodeling Your Home." Publication EPA/747/R94/002. April 1994. U.S. Environmental Protection Agency. Available from the National Center for Environmental Publications and Information — see contact information above.

Home*A*Syst Helps Ensure Your Safety

This *Home*A*Syst* handbook covers a variety of topics to help homeowners examine and address their most important environmental concerns. See the complete list of chapters in the table of contents at the beginning of this handbook. For more information about topics covered in *Home*A*Syst,* or for information about laws and regulations specific to your area, contact your nearest Cooperative Extension office.

Contact the National Farm*A*Syst/Home*A*Syst Office at: B142 Steenbock Library, 550 Babcock Drive, Madison, WI 53706-1293; phone: (608) 262-0024; e-mail: <HOMEASYST@MACC.WISC.EDU>.

This chapter was written by Karen Filchak, Extension Educator, University of Connecticut Cooperative Extension, Brooklyn, Connecticut.

► ACTION CHECKLIST ◄
Lead In and Around the Home: Identifying and Managing Its Sources

Write all high and medium risks below.	What can you do to reduce the risk?	Set a target date for action.
Sample: House was built in 1935. Paint has not been tested for lead.	Arrange for inspection of the condition of the paint. Test for lead-contaminated dust.	One week from today: April 3

Chapter 7 YARD AND GARDEN CARE

by K. Marc Teffeau, Wye Research and Education Center, University of Maryland Cooperative Extension and Ray Bosmans, Home and Garden Information Center, University of Maryland Cooperative Extension

If yours is like most homes, it is surrounded by lawns, gardens, shrubs, and trees that require regular maintenance. This chapter examines the potential impact of yard and garden care on the environment and your health. Topics covered include:

- Soil testing
- Lawn type and maintenance
- Fertilizers and pesticides
- Ground covers and erosion protection
- Composting
- Water conservation

Completing this chapter will help you identify and evaluate pollution risks and give tips for reducing those risks.

What are the environmental concerns?

Your yard and garden—the natural settings of your home and property—might be the last places you would look for pollution problems. But behind beautiful landscapes are activities that may threaten your health and the environment. On average, homeowners use ten times more chemical fertilizers and pesticides per acre than farmers use on farmland. Especially if applied improperly, these chemicals can find their way into drinking water wells and pollute nearby lakes and streams. Closer to home, children are particularly vulnerable to pesticides that are stored or used without proper safety precautions.

Other problems occur when exposed soil washes away during a storm, harming wildlife habitat and choking waterways. Indiscriminate watering of lawns and gardens wastes large amounts of water. Gasoline-powered mowers, weed cutters, leaf blowers, and other devices make noise and pollute the air. Powered by a two-cycle engine, a lawnmower in one hour spews the same amount of exhaust as a car driven 350 miles. While it may seem that your contribution to pollution is minor, the effects of chemicals, soil loss, and wasted water from hundreds or thousands of homes in your region can really add up.

Are you using your time and money effectively?

Americans spend a lot of money on garden gadgets, flowers, seeds, and chemical products. They also dedicate many hours of leisure time to caring for their yards and gardens. Valuable time and money may be wasted, however, if homeowners manage their lawns and gardens in an environmentally unsound way.

Think about the cost, time, and effort it would take to replace a lawn or garden damaged by over-fertilization or misuse of pesticides. Consider the hard work required to return unsightly, eroded areas back to productive use. Imagine how much less time lawn care would take if grass clippings were left on the lawn instead of being raked and bagged.

You can have a low-maintenance lawn without losing the well-kept appearance of your home. Good management practices not only benefit the environment —they can save you time and money as well.

Managing Your Lawns, Gardens, and Landscaping

Most homeowners desire a well-kept home landscape with attractive flowers, woody plants, and often a green lawn. A lot of time and money is spent to achieve this ideal, and the number of products and lawn-care services increases each year to meet the demand.

Normal applications of lawn and garden products generally pose few problems. A properly maintained home landscape, in fact, can help reduce soil erosion and increase water retention and soil fertility. Poor maintenance—either through neglect or excessive chemical use—can lead to soil problems, polluted runoff, and unsafe well water.

Look over the topics below, and read the ones that will help you better understand your yard and garden practices. Fill out the assessment table at the end to see where you might need to make improvements.

Has your soil been tested?

Adding fertilizer without first testing your soil is like taking medicine without knowing if you need it. Your soil already has some of the nutrients needed for good plant growth, such as nitrogen, phosphorus, and potassium. It is important to find out how much of each nutrient is present. Soil testing takes the guesswork out of how much fertilizer to use. Check with your local Cooperative Extension office, garden supply stores, and neighbors about testing your soil.

Testing often involves taking small samples from several places in your yard and garden. The soil is analyzed, and you receive a lab report that lists the amounts of each nutrient in each sample. Because of local differences, some parts of your property may need regular applications of fertilizer while other areas may need few or no applications. Soil tests should be conducted every three years.

What fertilizers are needed for your lawn?

Your soil tests will let you know if your lawn needs fertilizer, and if so, how much and where. Nitrogen is the key plant nutrient for building a thick, green lawn. Applied at the right time and in the right amount, fertilizers will supply the nitrogen your soil needs.

If you apply fertilizer at the wrong time or in the wrong amount, you may make conditions worse, and insect and disease problems can increase. Excess fertilizer is likely to wash away before the grass takes it up. Fertilizer in runoff contributes to unwanted plant growth in nearby streams or lakes. Especially in sandy soils, nitrogen and other chemicals can seep downward and enter groundwater used for drinking.

If you hire a lawn-care service, make sure they test your soil before applying fertilizer. Insist that lawn fertilizers only be applied when the weather is favorable — when rain is not expected for at least twenty-four hours. Be sure to keep children and pets away from treated lawns for at least twenty-four hours. Sweep excess fertilizer off of walks and back onto the lawn before it is washed away by rain. Nonchemical fertilizers, such as compost and fish meal, and other soil amendments also should be applied based on the needs of your lawn.

Are you taking proper care of your lawn?

It will be easier to keep your lawn healthy if the type of grass is suited to local growing conditions, which include rainfall amount, temperature, soil type, and available light. Contact your local Cooperative Extension office for a list of recommended grasses for your region.

Cutting your grass to the right height is important; lawns cut too short invite weeds to invade. Grass clippings should be left on the lawn—in many cases, they supply enough natural fertilizer so that only minimal additional fertilizer is needed to keep your lawn green and healthy. Clippings should be swept off of paved surfaces so they aren't carried away by stormwater.

Switching to a human-powered mower can cut down air and noise pollution and provide exercise. If you reduce your lawn size and grow plants that require little maintenance, such a mower can be practical. Consider using an electric mower for smaller-sized lawns.

Are you applying pesticides wisely?

Although removing weeds, insects, and other pests by hand is safest for the environment and your health, pesticides, if properly used, may pose only a minimal risk. The key is doing your homework before you start treatment. Correctly identifying the pest is the first step. Many plant problems are not caused by insects or disease but are related to temperature extremes, waterlogging or drought, damage caused by lawn mowers, or overuse of chemicals.

Learn when and where pesticides may be needed to control problems. Apply them only where pests occur. Select chemicals that are the least toxic or that break down quickly into less harmful substances. Check with your local Cooperative Extension office or garden supply stores for information. Remember to read the pesticide label carefully and follow the directions for application rates and methods.

Pest *prevention* is often simpler (and cheaper) than pest *removal*. If you have disease-resistant grasses or other plants and keep them healthy, pests will be less of a problem. Be sure to ask yourself, for the sake of clean groundwater and an environment with fewer chemical pollutants, if you can tolerate a few more weeds and "bugs" around your home.

Integrated pest management (IPM)

It sounds fancy, but integrated pest management, or IPM, is simply a systematic approach to controlling pests in your landscape. Although the use of nonchemical controls is preferred, chemicals may be used selectively if nothing else works. Weeds can be controlled by hand pulling (figure 7.1) or hoeing, and bugs can be removed by picking them off vegetables and garden plants. Cleaning up dead leaves and debris removes potential homes to pests. Using natural predators to control pests is another method; you can release into your garden beneficial insects and micro-organisms that feed on pest insects.

When you have no other choice, try to find nontoxic or low-toxic chemicals such as insecticidal soaps. Follow directions carefully, and mix only the amount you need. For IPM to work, you will have to give more time and attention to your yard and garden.

Do your landscape practices help prevent soil erosion?

Like pesticides and fertilizers, soil washed away by rain can pollute streams, lakes, or bays. Even if you do not live near water, soil will eventually be carried to surface water in runoff from storms. Gardens, lawns, and construction sites with areas of bare soil—especially on sloped land—are prone to soil erosion.

You can protect soil and reduce erosion by planting ground-cover vegetation or using wood-chip mulch or landscape fabric. On steep slopes, plant a vigorous ground cover but avoid turfgrass, which requires mowing. Building terraces or retaining walls on slopes can also help prevent soil loss. As with lawns, choose plants that are suited to your area and resistant to insects and diseases.

Do you make compost?

Composting is a cost-effective, natural way to handle leaves, grass clippings, and other yard wastes — materials that might otherwise end up in a landfill. Composting creates an organic, slow-release fertilizer and soil-enhancing material. It takes advantage of

Figure 7.1 Pull weeds by hand instead of controlling with chemicals.

nature's recycling system for breaking down plant and other organic materials.

To compost, simply put yard wastes in a pile, or install homemade or store-bought bins to contain the material. In addition to yard waste, you can add vegetable trimmings and fruit peels from your kitchen. Your compost pile will remain relatively odor-free if it is turned and aerated regularly (figure 7.2).

One word of caution: animal manures contain high levels of nitrogen, and different types of manures have different levels. If manure is left in piles exposed to the weather, nitrogen-rich runoff may result. If you

Figure 7.2 Compost piles will remain relatively odor-free if they are turned and aerated regularly.

mix manure from horses, sheep, cows, or other plant-eating animals into your compost, be sure to add plenty of high-carbon materials such as leaves, straw, or sawdust to keep concentrations of nitrogen and other nutrients low. This will help prevent contamination of groundwater. Do not put pet wastes (from cats and dogs) in compost piles because of potential parasite and disease problems. Try to locate piles at least 50 feet from any wells, lakes, or rivers.

Finished compost can be mixed into garden soil or spread on lawns as a slow-release fertilizer. Check with your local Cooperative Extension office, garden stores, the library, and your neighbors for other ideas.

Do your yard care practices save water?

The average American uses approximately 200 gallons of water each day. About half of that water may be used for landscaping and gardening, depending on climate, time of year, and plant species in the landscape. This is an immense amount of clean water — and only a small portion is actually used by your plants. If you convert your landscape plants to ones adapted to your region and climate, you will take the biggest step in conserving water.

In places with dry climates, there are many native plants that are drought-tolerant. Consider using drought-resistant turfgrass species like tall fescues and buffalo grass. Perennial flowers conserve water because their roots grow deeper than annual plants and require little or no watering once established. A shallow mulch (about 2 inches deep) of wood or bark chips over bare soil will reduce stormwater runoff and keep water from evaporating.

Watering wisely

Because most plants can tolerate at least short dry periods, watering should be timed to meet the biological needs of plants. Watering slowly and deeply helps develop deep roots; in the long run, your plants will need less frequent watering. The plants that seem to benefit most from shallow watering are the ones you don't want—weeds.

Plants can absorb only so much water. Overwatering wastes water and can injure certain plants. Placing several containers with 1-inch marks under your sprinkler will help you gauge how much water your lawn or garden is getting (figure 7.3).

Another option in some regions is to allow established cool-season lawn grasses to go dormant during the hot, dry summer rather than irrigating. Drip irrigation systems and soaker hoses deliver water to the intended plants efficiently. The time of day when you irrigate matters, too—early morning is best.

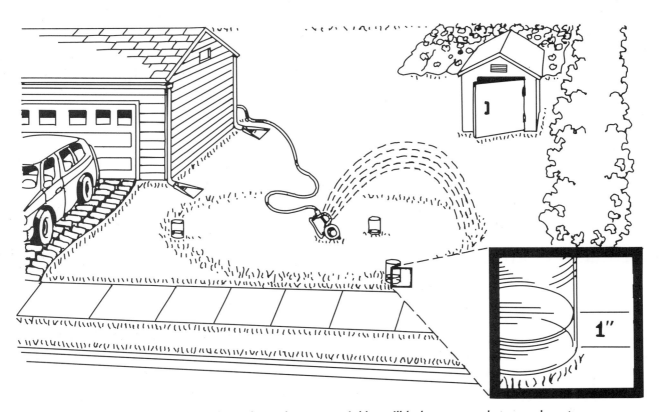

Figure 7.3 Placing containers with 1-inch marks under your sprinkler will help measure how much water you are applying.

Assessing your yard and garden care

The assessment table below will help you identify potential environmental risks related to your yard and garden maintenance practices. For each question, indicate your risk level in the right-hand column. Although some choices may not correspond exactly to your situation, choose the response that best fits. Refer to the previous pages if you need more information to complete the table.

Responding to risks

Your goal is to lower your risks. Complete the action checklist on the following page to help you make plans to reduce your risks.

▶ ASSESSMENT — Yard and Garden Care

	LOW RISK	MEDIUM RISK	HIGH RISK	YOUR RISK
Fertilizers	Soil is tested for nutrients, and fertilizer is used as recommended.	Soil is tested, but more fertilizer is used than recommended.	Soil is not tested, and fertilizer is used in large amounts.	❏ Low ❏ Medium ❏ High
Pesticides	Nonchemical or low-toxicity methods (such as integrated pest management) are used to control pests.	Chemicals are used according to label instructions.	Chemicals are used without regard to label instructions or conditions.	❏ Low ❏ Medium ❏ High
Lawn (turf) type and maintenance	Turfgrass is suited to soil type, available sunlight, and climate. Grass is pest-resistant and mowed to the proper height.	Turfgrass is suited to the site but is well-fertilized and mowed short.	Grass type is not suited to available light, soil type, or climate. Grass is pest-prone and mowed too short.	❏ Low ❏ Medium ❏ High
Ground cover and other plantings	Ground covers, flowers, trees, and shrubs are planted to reduce soil erosion. Plantings resist insects and disease.	A slow-spreading ground cover is used.	A hilly landscape or lack of ground cover causes soil erosion. Plants require insect- and disease-fighting chemicals to survive.	❏ Low ❏ Medium ❏ High
Composting	The compost pile is well-maintained: It is aerated regularly and contains yard waste, vegetable food scraps, and a nitrogen source such as manure.	The compost pile is poorly maintained: It is not aerated or lacks the proper mix of materials. Dog, cat, and other pet wastes are added to the pile.	The compost pile is poorly maintained: It contains excessive high-nitrogen material and is not turned regularly. The pile is less than 50 feet from a shallow well or surface water.	❏ Low ❏ Medium ❏ High
Water requirements of plants	Grass, flowers, trees, and shrubs are able to survive with normal rainfall.	Landscape plants require light to moderate watering.	Heavy watering is required to keep the lawn and other plants alive.	❏ Low ❏ Medium ❏ High
Watering methods	Watering is done in the morning or evening, only as needed. Low-water-use devices (like soaker hoses) are used. The sprinkler system is on manual control.	Watering is excessive. (For example: The sprinkler is left unattended, and much water lands on the pavement.)	Watering is done during the heat of the day. The sprinkler system is used daily without regard to weather conditions. There is excessive water runoff.	❏ Low ❏ Medium ❏ High

ACTION CHECKLIST

In the checklist below, write all medium- and high-risk practices you identified in the assessment table. For each risk, write down the improvements you plan to make. Use recommendations from this chapter and other resources to decide on actions you are likely to complete. A target date will keep you on schedule. You don't have to do everything at once, but try to eliminate the most serious risks as soon as you can. Often it helps to tackle the inexpensive actions first.

For More Information

Soil testing
Contact your local Cooperative Extension office or private testing laboratories. In your yellow pages, look under the heading "laboratories" or "soil testing."

Poison control centers
Write your state's toll-free number here:

_____

and keep it by your phone.

Home*A*Syst Helps Ensure Your Safety

This *Home*A*Syst* handbook covers a variety of topics to help homeowners examine and address their most important environmental concerns. See the complete list of chapters in the table of contents at the beginning of this handbook. For more information about topics covered in *Home*A*Syst*, or for information about laws and regulations specific to your area, contact your nearest Cooperative Extension office.

Contact the National Farm*A*Syst/Home*A*Syst Office at: B142 Steenbock Library, 550 Babcock Drive, Madison, WI 53706-1293; phone: (608) 262-0024; e-mail: <HOMEASYST@MACC.WISC.EDU>.

This chapter was written by K. Marc Teffeau, Regional Extension Specialist, Wye Research and Education Center, University of Maryland Cooperative Extension and Ray Bosmans, Regional Extension Specialist, Home and Garden Information Center, University of Maryland Cooperative Extension.

► ACTION CHECKLIST ◄
Yard and Garden Care

Write all high and medium risks below.	What can you do to reduce the risk?	Set a target date for action.
Sample: Fertilizers applied but soil has never been tested.	Find laboratory that does soil testing. Take samples and send them to lab.	One week from today: March 15

Chapter 8

LIQUID FUELS: Safe Management of Gasoline, Heating Oil, Diesel, and Other Fuels

by Richard Castelnuovo, National Farm*A*Syst Office, Madison, Wisconsin and Dean Solomon, Michigan State University Extension

L iquid fuels are used every day to power vehicles, run machines, and heat homes. This chapter helps you identify potential fuel-related risks to the environment and your family's health. It is divided into two parts:

1. *Portable Fuel Containers.* Fuel stored in portable containers and the gas tanks of gasoline-powered machines is a potential risk to groundwater and surface water. If you own any of the following, this part of the chapter applies to you:

   - lawn mower
   - chain saw
   - leaf blower or snow blower
   - weed trimmer
   - auxiliary generator
   - kerosene heater
   - snowmobile
   - camp stove
   - motorboat
   - automobile

2. *Aboveground, Underground, and Basement Storage Tanks.* This part of the chapter is for homeowners with aboveground, underground, or basement fuel tanks — active or inactive — on their property.* Topics discussed include:

   - tank location
   - tank management
   - tank removal and abandonment

   * *Applies to tanks that hold less than 1,100 gallons. Larger tanks or those used for business purposes may be subject to greater regulation. This chapter does not cover the storage of liquefied gases, such as liquid propane (LP) and liquid natural gas.*

What are the environmental and health concerns?

You may not have thought much about how you store gasoline, heating oil, and other fuels on your property. If you are like most people, you own at least one fuel-burning device such as a lawnmower and probably keep fuel in portable containers that hold 1 to 5 gallons. For home heating and vehicle use, you may also have larger quantities of fuel kept in underground, basement, or aboveground storage tanks.

Fuels are hazardous. Improperly managed, they can pollute the water you drink and the air you breathe. It is critical to prevent spills and leaks. As little as 1 gallon of gasoline can quickly contaminate groundwater above health advisory levels. Petroleum products contain many toxic compounds, including benzene, which is known to cause cancer.

You cannot depend on taste or smell to alert you about fuel in your drinking water. Contamination can come from unexpected sources. Unknown or forgotten underground tanks have come back to haunt property owners. Contaminated soil and water can rob your property of its value, trigger environmental liability and costly cleanups, and drive away lenders and property buyers. Vapors from fuel can ignite fires or collect underground and explode.

Fuel stored in large tanks poses greater risks of contamination than the small quantities stored for lawnmowers and similar equipment. While you should pay particular attention to high potential risks from large tanks, storing any amount of fuel increases the environmental risks around your home.

Improving fuel storage and management protects the health of your family, your community, and the environment. Better management can also safeguard your biggest investment—your home. This chapter can help you evaluate how you manage liquid fuels, identify areas of risk, and develop an action plan to reduce or eliminate potential problems.

PART 1 — Portable Fuel Containers

How much fuel do you buy and use?

It is best to purchase and store minimum amounts of fuel for short periods. This means (1) buying in small quantities and (2) buying no more than you need for a month or so of mowing the lawn or blowing snow.

Do you have more than a gallon of leftover fuel at the end of a season? Next time, buy less. If there are leftovers, try to use them up. Excess gasoline can be poured into a car's gas tank: Dilute one part old fuel with five parts new fuel to protect your engine. Leftover gasoline can also be given to a neighbor to use (figure 8.1). Beware of oil-blended fuels, which should be used only in engines designed for them. Fuel stabilizers may extend the shelf life of fuels.

Do you store fuels in approved containers?

It is important to use only safe, approved, or original sale containers to store fuels (figure 8.2). UL-approved containers (red for gasoline, blue for kerosene, and yellow for diesel) can be purchased in places as convenient as your local hardware store. The container should be clearly labeled to identify its contents and fitted with a spout or other device to allow pouring without spilling.

Storing fuels in an uncovered or unapproved container is dangerous. For an extra measure of spill protection, keep fuel containers inside a bucket or other container that can prevent leaks from spreading.

Figure 8.2 Use only UL-approved or original sale containers to store fuel. Storing fuel in an unapproved container, such as a glass jar or plastic jug, is dangerous.

Are containers kept in a well-ventilated, safe place?

To avoid fuel vapors — which are a health hazard and fire danger — keep fuel containers and fuel-powered devices in a secure, well-ventilated place with an impervious (paved) floor. Storage in an unattached shed or garage is safer than storage in a garage attached to your home or in a basement (figure 8.3). Store containers off the floor. Keep them out of the reach of children, and make sure the lids are tight to prevent easy access.

Do you check your fuel containers or machinery regularly?

Periodically check for leaks from storage containers and fuel-driven devices, especially if they haven't been used for some time. Small leaks can add up over time. You can keep on top of things through regular inspections and maintenance. Always recycle or safely dispose of engine maintenance products. (See chapter 5, "Managing Hazardous Household Products," for more information on disposal and recycling.)

Assessment 1 — Portable fuel containers

Check all the places where you store fuels — a garage, basement, or shed — and examine how fuels are stored. Use the assessment table on the following page to evaluate your practices. Some choices may not match your situation exactly, but answer the best you can. Refer to part 1 above if you need more information to complete the table.

Responding to risks

Your goal is to lower your risks. Turn to the action checklist on page 83 and record the medium- and high-risk practices you identified in the assessment table. Use the recommendations in part 1 to help you plan actions to reduce your risks. If you need more information, contact local fire officials.

Figure 8.1 If you have leftover fuel at the end of lawn-mowing season, a neighbor may be able to use it up.

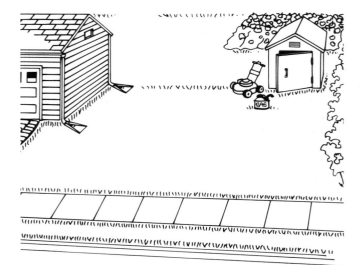

Figure 8.3 Storing fuel in an unattached shed or garage is safer than storing it in an attached garage or basement.

PART 2 — Aboveground, Underground, and Basement Storage Tanks

It is vital to know about fuel storage tanks on your property — including tanks that are currently in use and those that are abandoned. As a tank owner, you have many responsibilities and must keep up with increasingly strict laws. State law may require owners to register storage tanks with government authorities or restrict the use of certain tanks for residential purposes.

You are financially responsible for leaks from a tank on your property, even if you are unaware of the tank's existence. Standard homeowner's insurance does not typically cover the costly cleanups. Contact state environmental and health officials to learn more about your legal responsibilities.

▶ ASSESSMENT 1 — Portable Fuel Containers

	LOW RISK	MEDIUM RISK	HIGH RISK	YOUR RISK
Quantities stored	Moderate amounts of fuel are purchased. Fuel is stored for less than six months.	Fuel is stored more than six months before use.	Excess quantities of fuel are purchased. Fuel is stored more than twelve months.	❒ Low ❒ Medium ❒ High
Container safety	Fuel is stored in a UL-approved or original sale container.	Fuel is stored in a UL-approved or original sale container with signs of age or damage.	Fuel is stored in a non-approved container (for example, a glass jar or open container).	❒ Low ❒ Medium ❒ High
Storage location	Fuel is stored in a well-ventilated, unattached garage or shed away from the house. Concrete floor is best.	Fuel is stored in a garage attached to the house. The area is poorly ventilated.	Fuel is stored inside the home or in the basement. Dirt floor is least safe.	❒ Low ❒ Medium ❒ High
Management and disposal	Fuel is used up in devices, so disposal is unnecessary.	Fuel is stored on-site indefinitely or until evaporated.	Fuel is poured down a house drain or storm drain, poured on the ground, or sent to a landfill.	❒ Low ❒ Medium ❒ High
Leak detection	Storage containers and fuel-driven devices are examined often for leaks.	Storage containers and fuel-driven devices are sometimes examined for leaks.	Storage containers and fuel-driven devices are never examined for leaks.	❒ Low ❒ Medium ❒ High

Part 2 is divided into three sections: 2a, Tank Location; 2b, Tank Management; and 2c, Tank Removal and Abandoned Tanks. Review the information in each section, then answer the assessment questions that follow.

For the assessments in part 2, start by gathering basic information. How many tanks do you have and where are they located? **Assess each tank separately.** Using records or your memory, reconstruct the history of each tank. When was it installed? Has it been serviced or inspected? Unless you are certain you have no inactive underground tanks, it is best to check for them.

Part 2a — Tank location

This section covers both aboveground and underground tanks but not basement storage tanks. In the assessment table at the end of the section, answer only those questions that apply to you. Remember to assess each tank separately.

How far is your tank from wells and surface waters?
Fifty feet is the minimum recommended distance between your tank and nearby wells, but the greater the distance, the better. Other factors can influence the risk related to distance. Tanks are safer when located downslope (downhill) from wells. Certain soil types—such as sandy soils—allow pollutants to seep more rapidly into groundwater. The 50-foot minimum also applies to the distance from streams, wetlands, ponds, and other surface water. Some states and communities require greater minimum distances. Check with local officials for recommendations in your area.

For each high-risk tank, consider having a professional remove it or move it as far from wells and surface water as possible. If a tank must be near a well or surface water, aboveground tanks with secondary containment are preferred. Never try to convert an underground tank into an aboveground tank or vice versa. For professional assistance, look in the yellow pages under *tank, environmental, petroleum,* or *excavating.* If it is not possible to remove high-risk tanks, be extra careful to monitor them for spills and leaks.

What is the distance to the water table?
In most places, if you dig straight down, you will eventually reach water. This "water table" may be a few feet to hundreds of feet down. The distance to the water table is important for several reasons.

When water is close to the surface, there is greater chance for it to come in contact with the steel walls of a tank. In wet conditions, metal corrosion is more likely to occur. Some types of soil, especially clay, may also promote rusting.

Spills reach groundwater more quickly if the water table is close to the surface. Your tank may be exposed to similar water problems during flooding. You can get help finding out about your water table from agencies such as the state Geological Survey, the Natural Resources Conservation Service, or professionals such as well drillers. If you do not know how deep your underground tank is buried, assume it is no more than 10 feet. Again, for each high-risk tank, consider having a professional relocate or remove it. The cost of moving it today may be far less than paying for cleanup in the future.

Assessment 2a — Tank location
Evaluate your situation using the assessment table on the following page. Choose the response that best describes your situation. Refer to section 2a above if you need more information.

Responding to risks
Turn to the action checklist on page 83 to record medium- and high-risk practices. Use the recommendations in section 2a to help you plan actions to reduce your risks.

Part 2b — Tank management

This section deals with all three types of tanks (aboveground, underground, and basement). In the information below, review the parts that apply to the tanks you have.

Is your underground tank old and possibly leaking?
This is your highest concern. Buried tanks over fifteen years old have a dramatically higher chance of leaking. But even newer tanks and piping can leak, especially if they were incorrectly installed.

Corrosion protection helps keep steel tanks from leaking. Most older tanks do not have this protection and are at high risk for leaks. It is expensive to put corrosion protection on existing tanks, and it may be more cost-effective to replace unprotected tanks.

New underground tanks should—and in many states *must*—have corrosion protection such as an interior tank liner, a protective coating on the tank exterior, or cathodic (electric-chemical) protection. Fiberglass tanks do not corrode but are vulnerable to other problems, such as puncture by sharp objects.

Have you checked pipes and hoses?
The pipes, hoses, valves, and fittings connected to a storage tank can be a major source of leaks. They are often overlooked, especially if buried underground. Here, too, age is a factor. Piping fails because of corrosion, accidents, and weather-related factors such as

frost heaving. Professional installation and inspection is your key to avoiding problems.

How will you detect leaks?

Leak detection is more complicated for underground storage tanks and is critical for tanks older than fifteen years. Set up a schedule to regularly inspect all tanks for leaks and damage, including heating oil tanks in your basement.

One way to detect leaks is called "tank and pipe testing" or "tightness testing." This involves placing the tank, piping, and contents under pressure and checking for leaks. Many tank owners choose to have their underground tanks removed rather than pay for costly testing.

Do you keep track of fuel levels in the tank?

A less expensive way to check for leaks is to monitor the level of fuel over time. Measure precisely and record the amount of fuel in the tank each month. Then compare your records to the amount of fuel delivered and dispensed. Differences in your records may indicate a leak. This method is not always accurate, and small leaks will be missed. Underground tanks for heating fuel dispense automatically when in use and are best monitored in summer. If you suspect a problem, contact your local fuel supplier.

What signs of trouble should you look for?

Environmental changes. Your senses—sight, smell, and taste—are an important part of your leak detection plan. Is there an unexplained oil-like substance on streams or wet places near the tank? Is nearby soil stained with petroleum? Is there a strong and constant smell of petroleum near your tank? Have you or your neighbors smelled fuel odors near plumbing or sewer line openings, or in basements, or have you tasted it in your drinking water? Normally you can see leaks from an aboveground tank, but you should be aware of leaks in areas you cannot easily see, such as where the tank is in contact with the ground.

Mechanical changes. Be aware of unusual or changing operating conditions at the pump. Does your suction pump rattle, and does fuel flow unevenly? Does the pump hesitate too long before dispensing? These may be signs of leaks or damage to the piping.

What spill-protection actions have you taken?

Overfilling is the most common—and most avoidable—cause of spills. Never walk away while filling a vehicle with fuel. Close supervision of fuel transfers is one of your best forms of protection. Automatic shutoff devices are available to prevent spills but are not suitable for every tank. Spills resulting from overfilling basement (home heating fuel) tanks can be re-

WHO ARE YOU GOING TO CALL?

For more information on leak detection and for names of approved tank-testing methods and suppliers, contact local or state officials or a representative from a fuel marketing association.

► **ASSESSMENT 2a — Tank Location**

	LOW RISK	MEDIUM RISK	HIGH RISK	YOUR RISK
Distance from your well	The tank is greater than 100 feet from a water well.	The tank is between 50 and 100 feet from a water well.	The tank is less than 50 feet from a water well.	❏ Low ❏ Medium ❏ High
Distance from surface water	The tank is greater than 100 feet from a wetland, stream, river, pond, or lake.	The tank is between 50 and 100 feet from a wetland, stream, river, pond, or lake.	The tank is less than 50 feet from a wetland, stream, river, pond, or lake.	❏ Low ❏ Medium ❏ High
Water table level	The water table (distance to groundwater) is consistently more than 10 feet below the surface.	The water table is consistently between 5 and 10 feet below the surface.	The water table is consistently 5 feet or less below the surface.	❏ Low ❏ Medium ❏ High

duced by installing a vent whistle or fill-level indicator. Ask a tank or fuel supplier about these devices.

Box-like containment structures for aboveground tanks can prevent leaks and spills from spreading. Even if the entire contents of a tank leak, well-designed containment should keep the fuel and any water that has accumulated in the containment structure from escaping. You can construct a concrete dike and pad, or purchase special structures made for containment. Many states require a containment structure.

Is your fuel secure from theft?
Preventing access to your gasoline and diesel pumps protects against theft and lowers pollution risks. Unauthorized users can damage your tank or spill fuel. The simplest form of security is to lock your pump. Enclosing an aboveground tank within a 6-foot locked fence offers more security.

Are your tanks protected from accidents and damage?
Aboveground tanks can leak if they are not well-supported or protected from damage by vehicles and other objects. Tanks should be placed on a solid, stable base or on footings made of brick, cinder block, or concrete that resist changes in soil moisture and frost heaving. In your basement, do not store anything around or under a heating oil tank. Heavy objects can damage pipes. If your tank is located in a garage or outdoors, it needs to be protected from damage by your vehicle. If it is not enclosed in a structure, install posts or other barriers around it.

Assessment 2b — Tank management
Evaluate your situation using the table below. Read the left-hand column to see which questions apply to you. Indicate your risk level in the right-hand column. Refer to section 2b if you need more information.

▶ **ASSESSMENT 2b — Tank Management**

	LOW RISK	MEDIUM RISK	HIGH RISK	YOUR RISK
Age of your underground tank (gasoline, diesel, or heating oil)	Metal underground tank is less than fifteen years old and is protected from corrosion — OR — tank is synthetic (fiberglass).	Metal underground tank is less than fifteen years old and is not protected from corrosion.	Metal underground tank is more than fifteen years old.	❑ Low ❑ Medium ❑ High
Leak detection procedures (primarily for underground tanks)	Tank is regularly tested for "tightness," and monthly fuel use accounting is done.	Monthly fuel use accounting is done.	No testing or fuel use accounting is done.	❑ Low ❑ Medium ❑ High
Spill and overfill protection (for gasoline or diesel)	Filling is closely supervised.		Filling is unattended.	❑ Low ❑ High
Tank containment (aboveground tanks)	Tank is on a containment pad/dike capable of holding 125% of the tank volume.	Tank is on an impervious surface without a berm or dike for containment.	Tank has no protection to contain major leaks and spills.	❑ Low ❑ Medium ❑ High
Tank security (for gasoline or diesel)	Tank or pump is surrounded by a 6-foot locked fence, plus there is a lock on the pump.	Fill hose is locked (a requirement in most states).	No fence or enclosure is around the tank, and there are no locks.	❑ Low ❑ Medium ❑ High
Damage protection (aboveground and basement tanks)	Tanks and pumps are on stable concrete or steel supports. Tank is well-protected from damage by impact.		Tank is in contact with the ground or on poor footings. Tank is not well-shielded from impact.	❑ Low ❑ High

Responding to risks

Use the action checklist on page 83 to record the medium and high risks identified above. Use the recommendations in part 2b to help you plan actions to reduce your risks.

Part 2c — Tank removal and abandoned tanks

Unused tanks may pose potential risks to health, the environment, and financial assets (figure 8.4). Sometimes old pumps or fill pipes reveal the location of forgotten tanks. Former owners of the property, neighbors, or local fuel suppliers may be able to help.

What should you do with an abandoned tank?

Inactive tanks are an environmental threat until removed. Emptying and filling them with inert material like sand or soil is one solution, but it may not be permitted in your area.

Your best environmental and legal protection is to have the tank removed and the soil and groundwater checked for contamination. Your local fire marshal can tell you the best way to proceed.

You may need a permit to remove a tank or be required to hire a certified professional. Hiring a professional is highly recommended, even if you are legally allowed to remove your own tank. Every year this dangerous activity kills or injures nonexperts. Contractors can help you properly dispose of the tank at a landfill or with a scrap dealer.

What if contamination is discovered?

Tank owners may discover leaks when a tank is removed. Soil around and under a tank should be inspected for obvious signs of leaking — odors, stains, or visible fuel. If you suspect contamination, a more extensive site assessment should be promptly arranged.

Whenever you find a leak, it should be reported to local officials and state regulators who will expect you to respond to minimize harm to the environment. State funds may be available to help pay cleanup costs.

To protect yourself against legal claims, you should photograph and document all steps taken to remove a tank. Your written records should include: (1) state

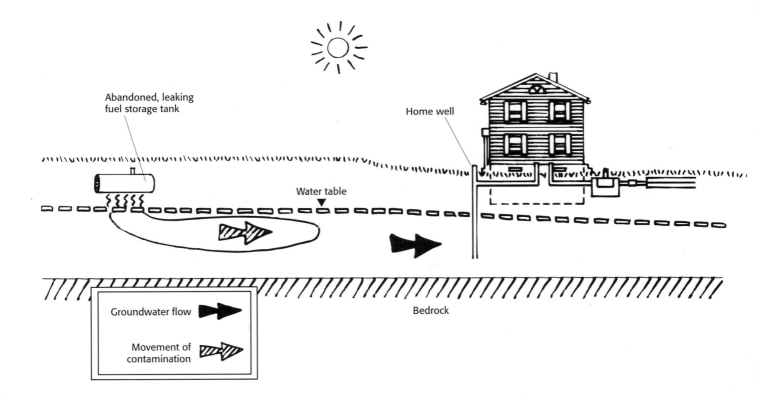

Figure 8.4 Abandoned fuel tanks on or near your property may be an unseen source of groundwater contamination.

agencies contacted, (2) the date the tank was filled or removed, (3) persons or companies who did the work, and (4) certified records that contamination was not found or, if it was found, detailed records of the resulting site examination.

Assessment 2c — Tank removal and abandoned tanks

If you have an abandoned or unused tank, evaluate your situation using the assessment table below. Indicate your risks in the right-hand column. Refer to section 2c above if you need more information.

Responding to risks

Use the action checklist on the following page to record your medium and high risks. Plan to take actions to reduce your risks.

ACTION CHECKLIST

When you finish the assessment tables, go back over the questions to ensure that all high and medium risks are recorded in the action checklist on the following page. For each of the risks, write down the improvements you plan to make. To help you decide what to do, use recommendations from this chapter as well as information from other resources.

Pick a target date that will keep you on schedule for making the changes. You don't have to do everything at once, but try to eliminate the most serious risks as soon as you can. Often it helps to start with inexpensive actions.

For More Information

Local and state contacts

Contact the agencies and organizations mentioned throughout this chapter, your nearest Cooperative Extension office, or a state office of natural resources or environmental protection. They should have publications to send and experts on staff to help answer your questions.

Publications

The U.S. Environmental Protection Agency (EPA) is a national clearinghouse for general information. The following EPA publication are available from the National Center for Environmental Publications and Information, P.O. Box 42419, Cincinnati, OH 45242-2419.

- "Guide to EPA Materials on Underground Storage Tanks." Order number EPA/510/B94/007.
- "Underground Storage Tanks: General Information Packet." Order number EPA/510/E93/001.

The World Wide Web (Internet)

A wealth of fuel storage tank information can be found on the World Wide Web (Internet). You can find web sites on this topic by using combinations of these terms in your searches: *petroleum, storage, tanks,* and *residential.*

▶ **ASSESSMENT 2c — Tank Removal and Abandoned Tanks**

	LOW RISK	MEDIUM RISK	HIGH RISK	YOUR RISK
Inactive tanks	Inactive tanks have been removed.	Inactive tanks have been left in place, emptied, and filled with approved material. *Caution:* This may be illegal in some areas!	Inactive tanks have been abandoned and left underground (or aboveground).	❏ Low ❏ Medium ❏ High
Inspection for contamination	Tank sites have been checked for signs of soil and groundwater contamination.		Tank sites have not been checked for signs of contamination.	❏ Low ❏ High

► ACTION CHECKLIST ◄
Liquid Fuels: Safe Management of Gasoline, Heating Oil, Diesel, and Other Fuels

Write all high and medium risks below.	What can you do to reduce the risk?	Set a target date for action.
Sample: Gas for lawnmower stored in a glass jug.	Buy a UL-approved container from the hardware store.	One week from today: May 15

Home*A*Syst Helps Ensure Your Safety

This *Home*A*Syst* handbook covers a variety of topics to help homeowners examine and address their most important environmental concerns. See the complete list of chapters in the table of contents at the beginning of this handbook. For more information about topics covered in *Home*A*Syst,* or for information about laws and regulations specific to your area, contact your nearest Cooperative Extension office.

Contact the National Farm*A*Syst/Home*A*Syst Office at: B142 Steenbock Library, 550 Babcock Drive, Madison, WI 53706-1293; phone: (608) 262-0024; e-mail: <HOMEASYST@MACC.WISC.EDU>.

This chapter was coauthored by Richard Castelnuovo, Staff Attorney, National Farm*A*Syst Office, Madison, Wisconsin and Dean Solomon, District Extension Natural Resources Agent, W. K. Kellogg Biological Station, Michigan State University Extension.

Chapter 9

INDOOR AIR QUALITY:
Reducing Health Risks and Improving the Air You Breathe

by Kathleen Parrott, Virginia Polytechnic Institute and State University

This chapter identifies where indoor air problems come from and what can be done to eliminate them. Health hazards related to air quality can be serious, but there are many opportunities for action. This chapter covers:

1. *Identifying and Controlling Potential Sources of Air Quality Problems*

   - Combustion byproducts, such as smoke and carbon monoxide
   - Building materials, including carpets, wood products, and paints
   - Household products and chemicals, such as cleaning solvents, adhesives, and paint strippers
   - Biological contaminants, like mildew, animal dander, and dust mites
   - Radon, a radioactive gas

2. *Ventilating Indoor Air*

   - Ventilation
   - Air cleaning

Completing this chapter will help you evaluate risks to your home's air quality and give tips for reducing those risks.

Why should you be concerned?

Clean air is a precious asset — fresh, full of oxygen, clean-smelling, and without harmful pollutants. If you are like most people, you spend at least half of your life inside your home. The air in many modern American homes, however, may not be fit to breathe. It can be more polluted and dangerous to your health than outdoor air. If your home has poor air quality, it may be simply annoying or unpleasant, or it may lead to serious health problems.

What are the signs of trouble?

It is not always easy to detect poor air quality. Although you can smell paint vapors and see smoke, many harmful pollutants, such as deadly carbon monoxide gas, are invisible and odorless. Common health problems, such as irritated eyes and nose, headaches, dizziness, tiredness, asthma, viral infections, and respiratory diseases may be due to substances in the air you breathe. Some serious effects of poor air quality, like lung cancer, may take many years to develop. People react differently to contaminants depending on their age, sensitivity, health status, and the type and length of exposure.

PART 1 — Identifying and Controlling Potential Sources of Air Quality Problems

Finding the source—or sources—of pollutants should be your first step. Addressing problems at the source is usually the most cost-efficient and effective approach. If you do nothing else, dealing with the most troublesome sources can lead to better health for everyone who breathes the air in your home. Poor air quality is usually not the result of a single pollutant. Reducing health risks to you and your family may require several actions.

Which sources exist in your home?

In addressing the problem of indoor air pollution, you need to think in terms of a specific pollutant, such as formaldehyde or carbon monoxide. You also have to track down the physical source of the pollutant—a furnace or damp crawl space, for example. This chapter cannot cover all possible pollutants and their sources, but it calls attention to the most common types and provides a starting point for investigation and action.

Part 1a — Combustion byproducts: what precautions are you taking?

Fuel-burning appliances

Airborne combustion byproducts come from oil and gas furnaces; wood and coal stoves; fireplaces; kerosene and gas space heaters; gas ranges, cooktops, and water heaters; and automobiles (figure 9.1). Pollutants include carbon monoxide, nitrogen and sulfur oxides, formaldehyde, and tiny breathable particles. These byproducts should be vented to the outside to prevent accumulation indoors. Never use unvented space heaters, gas stoves, or other combustion equipment in an enclosed room.

Carbon monoxide (CO) — an odorless, colorless gas — is a pollutant of special concern because it can kill. Symptoms of exposure such as headaches, dizziness, and nausea may be mistaken for other causes. A malfunctioning furnace or blocked flue pipe can result in fatal CO levels. Another dangerous source of CO is using a charcoal grill indoors.

CO detectors look and operate much like smoke detectors. Some experts recommend that CO detectors be installed in all homes that have combustion appliances. However, the detectors will not replace good maintenance of your heating system.

To determine the safety of your combustion appliances, call the dealer or a service professional for expert assistance. Yearly inspection of the equipment and chimney or flue is recommended for most heating systems. Like your car, your furnace needs cleaning and tune-ups to stay in good condition. Even a well-running system can become a hazard if the chimney or flue becomes blocked and gases cannot escape.

In addition, be alert for *backdrafting*. This occurs when the indoor air pressure is lower than outdoor air pressure, which causes combustion gases to be pulled back into the living space instead of being fully exhausted to the outside. Backdrafting is more likely in well-sealed, energy-efficient homes, especially when exhaust fans are in use. (See chapter 10, "Heating and Cooling Systems," for more information.)

Tobacco smoking

The smoke from cigarettes, cigars, and pipes contains a wide range of throat and lung irritants, as well as hazardous and cancer-causing chemicals. A smoky home environment puts everyone at risk, not just the smoker.

Assessment 1a — Combustion byproducts

Use the assessment table on the following page to rate your risks related to combustion byproducts. For each

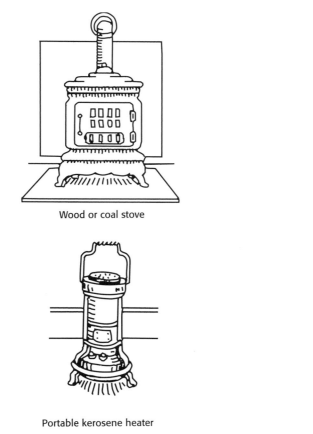

Wood or coal stove

Portable kerosene heater

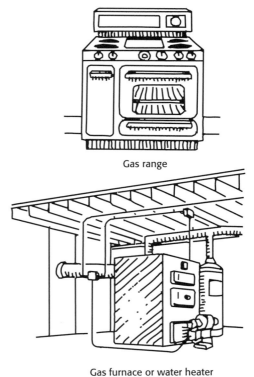

Gas range

Gas furnace or water heater

Figure 9.1 Examples of fuel-burning appliances and devices that may be present in a home.

question, indicate your risk level in the right-hand column. Although some choices may not correspond exactly to your situation, choose the response that best fits.

Responding to risks

Your goal is to lower your risks. Turn to the action checklist on page 94 to record the medium- and high-risk practices you identified. Use the information above to help you make plans to reduce your risks.

Part 1b — Which building materials, wood finishes, and home furnishings might be affecting your indoor air?

Many products used to build and furnish a home can pollute indoor air. Four of the most common types are discussed here: pressed wood products; carpet; paint, varnish, and other surface finishes; and asbestos. Especially when some of these materials are new, they can release hazardous emissions such as formaldehyde and other volatile organic compounds into the air. High temperatures and humidity can worsen the problem. Air pollutants can also come from old or deteriorating materials, such as asbestos.

Pressed wood products

Pressed or manufactured wood products made from wood chips or sawdust are widely used in home construction for flooring, sheathing, shelving, and cabinets. Furniture, too, is often made of manufactured wood products. The primary concern with pressed wood products is formaldehyde, which is used in the glues that hold these materials together. Formaldehyde will *off-gas*, or be released into the air, especially when a product is new. Some individuals are very sensitive to formaldehyde.

Sealing the surface of a wood product, especially the edges, will reduce formaldehyde emissions. Manufactured wood products that are formaldehyde-free or have low formaldehyde emissions (such as exterior-grade products) are available.

Carpet

New carpets can release volatile chemicals from carpet backing, padding, and fibers, as well as from the finishes that give carpeting its antistatic and soil-release properties. The carpet industry is working to reduce these emissions; the Carpet and Rug Institute

▶ ASSESSMENT 1a — Combustion Byproducts

	LOW RISK	MEDIUM RISK	HIGH RISK	YOUR RISK
Combustion appliances, venting	All combustion appliances are vented directly to the outside.	Unvented gas or kerosene heaters are used only in open spaces with a partially open window.	Kerosene or gas space heaters are frequently used in closed rooms.	❏ Low ❏ Medium ❏ High
Maintenance of combustion appliances, chimneys, and flues	Chimneys, flues, gas/oil furnaces, wood stoves, and other combustion appliances are inspected and cleaned at least once a year.	Chimneys, flues, gas/oil furnaces, wood stoves, and other combustion appliances have been inspected only once or twice in the past five years.	Chimneys, flues, and combustion devices are not inspected, or the inspection record is unknown.	❏ Low ❏ Medium ❏ High
Carbon monoxide detectors (only in homes with combustion appliances)	A carbon monoxide detector is properly installed, and the battery is tested weekly (if applicable).	A detector is installed, but the battery is not tested regularly (if applicable).	No carbon monoxide detector is installed.	❏ Low ❏ Medium ❏ High
Tobacco smoking	Tobacco smoking is not permitted in the home.	Smoking is permitted occasionally, but only in areas well-ventilated to the outside.	Frequent smoking causes smoky indoor air.	❏ Low ❏ Medium ❏ High

(CRI) now tests carpets for emissions (figure 9.2). Carpets of any age can act as a trap or sponge for chemical and biological pollutants that are carried in the air or tracked in from outside. Damp, dirty carpet is a breeding ground for biological pollutants. Carpets require regular vacuuming and cleaning.

Paint, varnish, and other surface finishes
Products used to finish, protect, and beautify materials in the home are potential sources of indoor air pollutants because they contain volatile organic compounds (VOCs). Products that are oil-, solvent-, or alkyd-based release more harmful vapors than water-based products. If you are not sure about a particular product, check the product label. If the instructions on the label say to clean up with soap and water, then the product is water-based.

Provide lots of extra ventilation when finishes are newly applied, or apply finishes outside the home and wait until they are dry to bring the finished product inside.

Lead, a highly toxic substance, was once a common ingredient in household paint. Many homes still have lead-based paint. Lead dust can be released into the air as the paint wears or during renovations. See chapter 6, "Lead In and Around the Home," for more information.

Asbestos
Until about 1980, asbestos was widely used in building materials to give strength, increase heat insulation, and provide fire resistance. It was used in roof

---

PLANNING TO INSTALL A NEW CARPET?

For better air quality, try to:

1. Choose a carpet that is certified by CRI as a low-emissions carpet.

2. Ask the carpet dealer to unroll the carpet and leave it in a well-ventilated area for at least twenty-four hours before it is brought to your home.

3. Plan to install the carpet at a time of year when you can provide extra ventilation by opening windows during and for several days after installation.

4. Arrange for chemically sensitive persons to be out of the house for the first few days after the new carpet is installed.

5. Thoroughly vacuum the old carpet before removal to minimize dust and biological pollutants in the air.

---

and siding shingles, floor tiles, soundproofing materials, insulation around pipes, heating ducts and flues, and decorative finishes. When asbestos products get old, they can become crumbly and disperse tiny fibers into the air. If you breathe asbestos particles over time, they can accumulate in your lungs and lead to serious respiratory problems.

Assessment 1b — Building products and furnishings
Use the table on the following page to identify risks related to building product emissions and asbestos. For each question, indicate your risk level in the right-hand column. Although some choices may not correspond exactly to your situation, choose the response that best fits.

Responding to risks
Your goal is to lower your risks. Turn to the action checklist on page 94 to record the medium- and high-risk practices you identified. Use the recommendations above to help you reduce your risks.

Part 1c — Biological contaminants: how do they affect indoor air?
Your house is home to many organisms. Some are wanted, like pets, but many are uninvited. Biological contaminants come from living or once-living organisms. They include mainly animal hair, dander, saliva, and feces; molds and other fungi; dust mites; insect residues; pollen; and microscopic organisms. These can cause odors, damage household materials, lead

---

INDOOR AIR QUALITY CONSUMER INFORMATION

IMPORTANT HEALTH INFORMATION:
SOME PEOPLE EXPERIENCE ALLERGIC OR FLU-LIKE SYMPTOMS, HEADACHES, OR RESPIRATORY PROBLEMS WHICH THEY ASSOCIATE WITH THE INSTALLATION, CLEANING, OR REMOVAL OF CARPET OR OTHER INTERIOR RENOVATION MATERIALS. IF THESE OR OTHER SYMPTOMS OCCUR, NOTIFY YOUR PHYSICIAN OF THE SYMPTOMS AND ALL MATERIALS INVOLVED.

SENSITIVE INDIVIDUALS
PERSONS WHO ARE ALLERGY-PRONE OR SENSITIVE TO ODORS OR CHEMICALS SHOULD AVOID THE AREA OR LEAVE THE PREMISES WHEN THESE MATERIALS ARE BEING INSTALLED OR REMOVED.

NOTE:
YOU CAN REDUCE YOUR EXPOSURE TO MOST CHEMICAL EMISSIONS WHEN CARPET AND OTHER INTERIOR RENOVATING MATERIALS ARE INSTALLED, CLEANED, OR REMOVED BY INCREASING THE AMOUNT OF FRESH AIR VENTILATION FOR AT LEAST 72 HOURS. (See Installation and Maintenance Guidelines or ask for Owner's Manual.)

INSTALLATION GUIDELINES:
- VACUUM OLD CARPET BEFORE REMOVAL
- VACUUM FLOOR AFTER CARPET AND PAD HAVE BEEN REMOVED
- ALWAYS VENTILATE WITH FRESH AIR (OPEN DOORS AND/OR WINDOWS, USE EXHAUST FANS, ETC.) DURING ALL PHASES OF INSTALLATION AND FOR AT LEAST 72 HOURS THEREAFTER
- IF ADHESIVES AND/OR PAD ARE USED, REQUEST THOSE WHICH HAVE LOW CHEMICAL EMISSIONS
- FOLLOW DETAILED INSTALLATION GUIDELINES FROM MANUFACTURER OR FROM CARPET AND RUG INSTITUTE

The manufacturer of this carpet participates in a program which seeks to develop ways to reduce emissions by testing samples of carpet. With fresh air ventilation, most carpet emissions are substantially reduced within 48-72 hours after installation.

INDOOR AIR QUALITY CARPET TESTING PROGRAM
product type:

FOR MORE INFORMATION: CARPET AND RUG INSTITUTE 800/882-8846

Figure 9.2 Carpet and Rug Institute (CRI) label that appears on carpet tested for low emissions.
Reprinted with permission from the Carpet and Rug Institute.

	LOW RISK	MEDIUM RISK	HIGH RISK	YOUR RISK
New building materials, paints, varnishes, and furnishings	Low- or no-emission furnishings, building materials, paints, and varnishes are selected. New items are given adequate ventilation or sealed.	New furnishings, building materials, paints, and varnishes are given increased ventilation.	There is no attempt to select low-emission products, and ventilation is inadequate.	❏ Low ❏ Medium ❏ High
Carpet	Low-VOC carpet is selected and aired before and during installation. Carpet is vacuumed regularly using a vacuum cleaner with a high-efficiency filter; spills are cleaned immediately.	New carpet is installed without ventilation.	Old carpet is poorly maintained.	❏ Low ❏ Medium ❏ High
Asbestos (in homes built before the 1980s)	Asbestos is present but safely encased and isolated. Areas with asbestos are checked regularly.	Asbestos is present and intact but located in high-traffic areas.	Asbestos-containing material is in poor shape and crumbling. People are exposed to the dust and fibers.	❏ Low ❏ Medium ❏ High

to allergic reactions, and cause infectious diseases and respiratory problems. Each person has a different sensitivity to these contaminants.

Biological pollutants are found in every home and cannot be eliminated completely. Their growth and quantities can be controlled, however, by keeping surfaces clean and moisture levels low (see sidebar). Many biological contaminants will increase in damp or humid spaces. Good maintenance practices can control moisture and reduce the need for chemical products like pesticides and disinfectants — both of which could add other pollutants to the air.

Dust control
Household dust includes some biological contaminants that are common allergens. Animal dander is shed from skin, hair, or feathers. Dust mites are microscopic insects, and their feces—the primary allergen—are easily airborne. Regular cleaning, including dusting with a treated cloth, damp cleaning, and laundering bedding with hot water, are needed to control these contaminants.

Regular vacuum cleaning may help control dust, but some particles are so small that they pass through cleaner filters and become airborne. Some vacuum

TIPS FOR CONTROLLING MOISTURE IN THE HOME

- Prevent standing water, such as in basements or the drip pans of refrigerators and air conditioners.

- Fix leaks and seepage problems immediately.

- Make sure rainwater drains away from your house.

- Use a vapor-proof ground cover (such as 4- to 6-mil plastic) in enclosed crawl spaces.

- Use fans that exhaust to the outside when bathing, showering, or cooking.

- Vent all combustion appliances to the outside.

- Use dehumidifiers and/or air conditioners to remove excess moisture in warm, humid weather.

- Avoid oversized air conditioners.

- Limit the use of humidifiers.

- Limit houseplants.

cleaners have high-efficiency (HEPA) filters to trap more particles (figure 9.3).

If dust-related allergies are a particular problem, limit the use of carpeting, upholstered furnishings, and "dust catchers" such as window blinds and knick-knack displays. Follow recommended procedures for dust control, and keep sleeping areas as allergen-free as possible.

Assessment 1c — Biological contaminants
Use the table below to identify risks related to air pollution from biological sources. For each question, indicate your risk level in the right-hand column. Although some choices may not correspond exactly to your situation, choose the response that best fits.

Figure 9.3 Vacuum cleaners with high-efficiency (HEPA) filters trap more particles.

Responding to risks
Your goal is to lower your risks. Turn to the action checklist on page 94 to record the medium- and high-risk practices you identified. Use the recommendations above to help you make plans to reduce your risks.

Part 1d — Household chemical products and radon

Household chemical products: what types of air quality problems do they cause?
You may use a variety of potentially hazardous chemical products in your home — for maintenance, cleaning, personal grooming, and hobbies. Some products, such as those from spray cans, can release chemicals or particles into the air during use. Others emit chemicals as the product dries or cures (such as glues and caulking) or from off-gassing as the product ages (plastics and air fresheners, for example). Potentially hazardous products include furniture waxes, paint strippers, adhesives, some cleaning products, disinfectants, degreasers, cosmetics, and hobby supplies.

Products having petroleum distillates or other volatile organic compounds (VOCs) create more unhealthy emissions than water-based products. Many "everyday" household products such as chlorine bleach, ammonia, boric acid, and deodorizers may generate indoor air pollutants *if used improperly.* Some household products contain pesticides and other toxic chemicals and require special precautions. See chapter 5, "Managing Hazardous Household Products," for more on this topic.

Reducing the hazard from household products
Choose the least hazardous product and the smallest amount that will do the job. Always follow label di-

▶ ASSESSMENT 1c — Biological Contaminants

	LOW RISK	MEDIUM RISK	HIGH RISK	YOUR RISK
Dust control	House is cleaned regularly. No furry pets are kept in the home. Little or no carpeting is in the home.	Furry pets live in the home, but the house is cleaned regularly.	Pet hair and dust are allowed to accumulate in living and sleeping areas. House is mostly carpeted, and carpet is poorly maintained.	❏ Low ❏ Medium ❏ High
Moisture control	There is no evidence of condensation in high-moisture areas or seasonally. Excess moisture is vented to the outside.	There is evidence of condensation in high-moisture areas or seasonally. Exhaust fans are sometimes used.	Damp air is not exhausted. Crawl space does not have a ground cover or vents. There are leaks, drips, or standing water in, around, or under the house.	❏ Low ❏ Medium ❏ High

rections and provide adequate ventilation (figure 9.4). To avoid having to store hazardous products, buy only the amount you will need, then use it up. Give away leftovers or properly dispose of household chemicals that are not needed. You can reduce the need for many household chemicals by practicing preventive maintenance, such as giving quick attention to spills and stains or promptly removing food wastes to control odors and pests.

Radon: Is it present in your home?
Radon is a naturally occurring radioactive gas found in rocks and soil in many areas. It enters the home through cracks and openings that are in contact with the ground — in a basement, for example (figure 9.5). Radon is invisible, has no odor, and causes no immediate symptoms or health effects. It is, however, a cause of lung cancer. Smokers are especially at risk if radon is present.

Different parts of the country have different levels of radon. If you live in a high-risk area for radon, or if

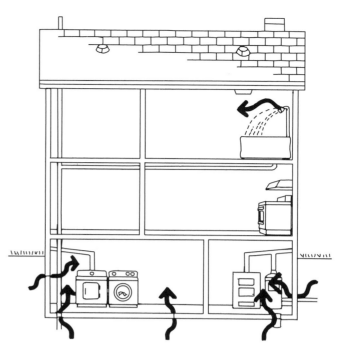

Figure 9.5 Radon gas enters a home through openings in contact with the ground and in household water.

neighbors have found high levels, you should take this potential threat seriously. Because every home is built differently, even neighboring homes can have very different levels. The only way to find out about radon in your home is by testing. The generally recommended level of radon, in the United States, is below 4 picoCuries per liter (pCi/L) of air.

Radon testing and treatment
Look for radon test kits that say "meets EPA requirements." An inexpensive screening test that lasts four to seven days and costs $5 to $10 can give a rough idea of how much radon is present. The test should be conducted when windows and doors are closed. If a high level of radon is found, a second long-term test (at least three months' duration) is recommended to give more accurate information about radon in the home.

If an unsafe level of radon is verified by the second test, there are a variety of things you can do to reduce radon. These involve either plugging the leaks—such as caulking cracks in basement walls—or changing the ventilation patterns of your home so that radon isn't drawn inside. Check with your state radon office, Cooperative Extension, local contractors, or health agencies for advice. A trained and certified radon mitigator can be invaluable in helping you reduce radon in your home. If you plan to sell your home, check local and state laws to see if radon testing and treatment are required.

Figure 9.4 Provide adequate ventilation when using hazardous household products.

Assessment 1d — Household products and radon

Use the table below to identify risks related to household chemical products and radon. For each question, indicate your risk level in the right-hand column. Although some choices may not correspond exactly to your situation, choose the response that best fits.

Responding to risks

Your goal is to lower your risks. Turn to the action checklist on page 94 to record the medium- and high-risk practices you identified. Use the recommendations above to help you make plans to reduce your risks.

PART 2 — Ventilating Indoor Air

The removal or reduction of pollution sources is the first priority in improving the air quality in your home. The second priority is to dilute the concentration of air pollutants through increased ventilation of the home.

Even in homes with few sources of contamination, ventilation is needed, especially during seasons when windows and doors are kept shut. Many homes "leak" air, which may help maintain freshness but wastes energy. Newer homes tend to have tighter construction, which makes it easier for pollutants to build up to dangerous levels. Tight homes may also be susceptible to humidity problems.

How well is your house ventilated?

Use your nose and eyes to help evaluate indoor air quality. Be aware of persistent odors of chemicals, mildew, or tobacco smoke. Steamy windows in cool weather indicate high levels of moisture in the home. (See "Tips for Controlling Moisture in the Home" on page 89.) Lingering odors of grease and food may mean that your kitchen needs more ventilation.

Home ventilation is usually measured in air changes per hour (ACH). This is a measure of how many times per hour the volume of air in your home is replaced with outdoor air. Many factors can affect the ACH rate, including the structure of the home; weather; opening or closing of doors and windows; heating, cooling, and ventilating equipment; and use of fans.

A blower door test administered by a professional is needed to adequately measure ventilation rates in your home. A blower door consists of a large fan mounted in a frame that is temporarily installed in an outside doorway. The fan forces air into or out of the home. Pressure readings obtained from the test help in calculating air leakage and the ACH rate. The test can also help determine where leakage is occurring.

▶ **ASSESSMENTS 1d — Household Products and Radon**

	LOW RISK	MEDIUM RISK	HIGH RISK	YOUR RISK
Household products and chemicals	Products with hazardous vapors are avoided or used only outdoors or indoors with proper ventilation and safety precautions. Hazardous products are not stored in the home.	Products with hazardous vapors are used indoors with some ventilation. Only short periods of exposure occur.	Products with hazardous vapors are used indoors without ventilation. Long periods of exposure occur. Hazardous products are stored in the home.	❐ Low ❐ Medium ❐ High
Radon	A radon test was conducted properly, and the radon level is below the threshold for action.	Radon is present at or near the threshold for action.	Radon is present in excess of acceptable levels — OR — radon level is unknown, no testing has been done.	❐ Low ❐ Medium ❐ High

Increasing the ventilation rate of your home will reduce the concentration of air pollutants. Exhaust fans in kitchens and bathrooms are helpful, as long as adequate replacement air is available. Some ventilation equipment can increase ventilation while conserving energy. For example, a heat recovery ventilator removes "stale" air from a house and brings in fresh air. The incoming fresh air is warmed by heat removed from the outgoing air. If you suspect the ventilation in your home is inadequate, consult an energy professional.

What about air filters and air cleaners?

Air filters in your heating/cooling air circulation system need to be inspected regularly and replaced or cleaned when dirty. Dirty or clogged filters will limit the efficiency of the equipment. Standard air filters on heating and cooling equipment will remove only the largest dust particles. Other high-efficiency filters are more effective and will remove particles such as dust, smoke, pollen, and some microorganisms. Gases will generally go right through air filters.

There are several types of air cleaners, based on the different ways they clean the air. Mechanical filters are made of fibers or pleated filter papers that trap small particles as air passes through. Electrostatic air cleaners use an electrical field to attract charged airborne particles; ion generators are used to give particles a charge that makes them "stick" to surfaces in the home. Solid sorbent cleaners — such as activated carbon or charcoal — can capture gaseous pollutants.

NOTE

Remember that air filters and cleaners are of limited use in solving indoor air quality problems. If poorly maintained, they could actually contribute to your air quality problems. The effectiveness of filters and air cleaners depend on several things:

- the contaminants removed from the air
- how much air passes through the device
- the kinds of airborne particles in your air
- where the unit is located in relation to the source of pollutant
- regular maintenance of the system

Assessment 2 — Ventilating indoor air

Use the table below to identify risks related to air freshness. For each question, indicate your risk level in the right-hand column. Although some choices may not correspond exactly to your situation, choose the response that best fits.

Responding to risks

Your goal is to lower your risks. Turn to the action checklist on the following page to record the medium- and high-risk practices you identified. Use the recommendations above to help you make plans to reduce your risks.

▶ ASSESSMENT 2 — Ventilating Indoor Air

	LOW RISK	MEDIUM RISK	HIGH RISK	YOUR RISK
Air freshness	Indoor air usually smells clean, in all seasons. Extra ventilation is provided as needed.	Air sometimes has an odor or mustiness, especially during certain times of the year.	Air nearly always smells musty, damp, acrid, smoky, heavy, or like "chemicals."	❏ Low ❏ Medium ❏ High
Ventilation	House is well-ventilated. Exhaust fans are used in the kitchen and bathroom.	"Leaky" house gives some uncontrolled ventilation.	House is poorly ventilated. No kitchen/bath exhaust fans are used.	❏ Low ❏ Medium ❏ High

ACTION CHECKLIST

Go back over the assessment tables and find the high and medium risks you identified. Make sure they are recorded in the checklist. For each medium and high risk listed, write down the improvements you plan to make. Use recommendations from this chapter and other resources to decide on an action you are likely to complete. A target date will keep you on schedule. You don't have to do everything at once, but try to eliminate the most serious risks as soon as you can. Often it helps to tackle the inexpensive actions first.

► ACTION CHECKLIST ◄
Indoor Air Quality: Reducing Health Risks and Improving the Air You Breathe

Write all high and medium risks below.	What can you do to reduce the risk?	Set a target date for action.
Sample: Chimney and furnace not given a "tune-up" for several years.	Call heating/cooling expert to inspect, clean, and tighten the system.	One week from today: September 1

For More Information

Radon testing

Check the test kits at hardware and building supply stores, or contact your local or state health department or environmental agency, a Cooperative Extension office, or private testing laboratories. Recorded information about radon is available twenty-four hours a day from the National Radon Hotline. Call (800) SOS-RADON.

Resources

- Indoor Air Quality Information Clearinghouse (IAQ INFO). Call toll-free (800) 438-4318, Monday–Friday, 9:00A.M.–5:00P.M. EST. Or write to them at PO Box 37133, Washington, DC 20013-7133. Ask for their list of currently available documents.

- Clean Air Council, (215) 567-4004, 135 South 19th Street, Philadelphia, PA 19103. Call for information on services, where to get more information, and testing procedures.

- American Lung Association. Contact your local organization or call (800) LUNG-USA toll-free.

- Carpet and Rug Institute, Indoor Air Quality Testing Program, (800) 882-8846 toll-free or (706) 278-3176. Or write PO Box 2048, Dalton, GA 30722-2048.

Publications

- "The Inside Story: A Guide to Indoor Air Quality," a 36-page, illustrated publication by the U.S. Environmental Protection Agency. Identifies problems and control methods for indoor air pollutants including radon, tobacco smoke, lead, and household products. Applies to all regions of the United States. Cost is $44 per package of twenty-five. Order from Superintendent of Documents, PO Box 371954, Pittsburgh, PA 15250-7954, or fax your order to (202) 512-2250. Mention order processing code #3136. Single copies can be requested from the Indoor Air Quality Information Clearinghouse (see contact information above under "Resources").

- "Household Care Products and Indoor Air Quality" (pamphlet). Free single copies are available from Chemical Specialties Manufacturers Association, Attn. CTIF, 1913 Eye Street NW, Washington, DC 20006. Product order number is CP-6.

Home*A*Syst Helps Ensure Your Safety

This *Home*A*Syst* handbook covers a variety of topics to help homeowners examine and address their most important environmental concerns. See the complete list of chapters in the table of contents at the beginning of this handbook. For more information about topics covered in *Home*A*Syst*, or for information about laws and regulations specific to your area, contact your nearest Cooperative Extension office.

Contact the National Farm*A*Syst/Home*A*Syst Office at: B142 Steenbock Library, 550 Babcock Drive, Madison, WI 53706-1293; phone: (608) 262-0024; e-mail: <HOMEASYST@MACC.WISC.EDU>.

This chapter was written by Kathleen Parrott, Associate Professor and Extension Housing Specialist, Virginia Polytechnic Institute and State University.

Chapter 10

HEATING AND COOLING SYSTEMS: Saving Energy and Keeping Safe

by Lori S. Marsh, Department of Biological Systems Engineering, Virginia Polytechnic Institute and State University

This chapter helps you identify possible problems with your home heating system, duct system, and the house *envelope* (the foundation, floors, walls, ceilings, and roof). By keeping your system in proper order, you can avoid unhealthy situations, reduce energy bills, increase your comfort level, and prevent structural damage. This chapter covers:

1. *Combustion Heating Appliance Ventilation Safety*

2. *Energy Consumption*

3. *Energy Efficiency* (heating/cooling systems, air-sealing and insulation, and domestic hot water)

What do you expect from your house?

Your house should be a safe, comfortable place that is affordable and durable. How a home is constructed, insulated, and heated and cooled directly affects how it meets these objectives. A house is affordable only when costs for heating and cooling are reasonable. Energy bills are lowest if a home is tightly air-sealed and properly insulated and if all mechanical systems are operating efficiently. (Before extensively air-sealing your home, it is critical to ensure that doing so will not cause health or moisture problems. See part 3b, which begins on page 100, for more information.) *Above all else, your home must be a healthy place to live.*

PART 1 —Combustion Heating Appliance Ventilation Safety

If your furnace, wood stove, boiler, or water heater burns gas, oil, wood, or coal, it is important that the venting system, which carries combustion gases out of the house, is properly functioning. (This also applies to a gas clothes dryer.) Part 1 explains how venting systems work and what will keep them safe. At the end of part 1, fill out the assessment table to identify potential risks with your system.

Are your combustion appliances safe?

When fuel (gas, oil, coal, or wood) is burned, carbon dioxide and water vapor are given off. If the burner is not functioning perfectly, carbon monoxide and other harmful pollutants are also produced (see chapter 9, "Indoor Air Quality," for more information about combustion byproducts). Most combustion appliances are vented to remove combustion byproducts from the home. However, improper maintenance can lead to problems such as blocked vents (Where did that bird put its nest?) and cracked flues. Vents or flues should be checked annually to make sure they are in good working order.

The three types of venting systems are natural-draft, power-vented, and sealed-combustion. Natural-draft or atmospheric-vent systems rely on the natural tendency of warm gases to rise. Natural-draft appliances always vent into a vertical flue (either masonry or metal) and have a draft hood, which draws extra indoor air into the flue.

Natural-draft appliances are particularly susceptible to *backdrafting*. This problem occurs when exhaust equipment such as a clothes dryer, central vacuum, or exhaust fan draws air out of a house, creating a negative pressure within the house. This can cause combustion byproducts to *backdraft,* or be pulled into the house instead of going out the vent (figure 10.1).

With power-vented systems, a small blower exhausts combustion byproducts from the house. Flue gases from power-vented appliances rarely backdraft.

The newest furnaces and water heaters use sealed-combustion systems. With this type of system, air needed for combustion is brought in from outside through an intake pipe. Flue gases are vented outside through a second pipe. No chimney is needed. These systems are completely isolated from inside air, and as long as the intake and vent pipes are not blocked

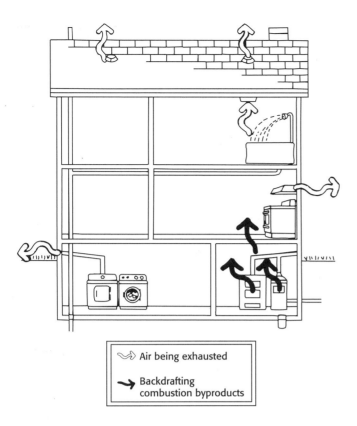

	Air being exhausted
	Backdrafting combustion byproducts

Figure 10.1 Backdrafting occurs when exhaust fans lower in-home air pressure.

or damaged, sealed-combustion appliances are immune to backdrafting.

Unvented appliances, including gas fireplace logs, should only be used in well-ventilated areas. If you must use unvented appliances, open a window in the room at least 1 inch.

Do your appliances get enough air?
For safe operation, it is critical that combustion appliances have enough air to work properly. The National Fire Protection Association (NFPA) codes (or more stringent local codes) must be followed to ensure safe installation and operation of combustion equipment.

Sealed-combustion units draw air directly from outside the home. However, natural-draft and power-vented units draw air from the indoor space in which they are located. If you have combustion equipment in a closet or other confined space, make sure the appliance gets enough air. This is often accomplished with louvered doors. Do not place anything inside or outside of the confined space that might block air flow.

Assessment 1 — Combustion heating appliance ventilation safety
If you have a combustion appliance, complete the table below. For each question, indicate your risk in the right-hand column. Some choices may not correspond exactly to your situation, so choose the response that best fits. Refer to part 1 if you need more information.

▶ **ASSESSMENT 1 — Combustion Heating Appliance Ventilation Safety**

	LOW RISK	MEDIUM RISK	HIGH RISK	YOUR RISK
Vent system for combustion appliances	All combustion appliances have sealed-combustion venting systems.		Unvented space heaters or gas logs are used. —OR— Vent pipes are showing signs of damage. —OR— Rust or carbon is present on top of an appliance or below the draft hood.	❏ Low ❏ High
Condition of chimney or flue	The chimney or flue is inspected annually.	The chimney or flue has been inspected only once in the past five years.	The chimney or flue has not been inspected, or the inspection record is unknown.	❏ Low ❏ Medium ❏ High
Air for combustion (does not apply to sealed-combustion appliances)	Combustion equipment is in a well-ventilated space (for example, an attic or garage) or a basement with adequate combustion air.	Combustion equipment is in a well-sealed basement. (This is a higher risk if an exhaust, such as from a clothes dryer, is in the same space.)	Combustion equipment is in a small space (for example, a closet), and openings are blocked.	❏ Low ❏ Medium ❏ High

Responding to risks

Your goal is to lower your risks. Turn to the action checklist on page 105 and write down the high and medium risks you identified. Refer to the information in part 1 to help you make plans to reduce your risks.

PART 2 — Energy Consumption

The amount of energy consumed in your home depends on many factors, including how well the home is insulated, the efficiency of appliances and equipment, the local weather and climate, and your lifestyle. This section describes how to calculate your energy use and determine if it is high or low. At the end of this section, fill out the equations in assessment 2. If your energy consumption is low, that's good news. If it is high, or if there are ways you could save more energy (and money), continue to part 3.

Does your house use too much energy?

Figure 10.2 shows how energy is used in the typical American home. Your family's lifestyle will affect how energy is consumed in your home.

The best and most accurate way to determine the energy efficiency of your home is to have a home energy audit done by a service professional. Without an audit, it is not easy to know if your energy consumption is "too much." Contact your local utility to see if they offer a residential energy audit or can provide data on average energy consumption for houses similar to yours. Alternately, you can ask them to quote you a monthly payment plan that will indicate the average energy consumption for a house in your geographic location.

When you call, be sure to describe your energy and fuel uses. For example, you may have an all-electric home, or you may heat with gas and cook with electricity. It is also important to specify whether or not you have air conditioning. Make sure the utility understands that you are trying to determine typical energy usage for a home the size of yours. Otherwise, they may quote you a monthly payment plan based on your past energy usage.

Assessment 2 — Energy consumption

Use the equations in the assessment on the following page to evaluate whether your energy costs are high or low. First, check your records or call your utility to determine how much you spent on energy bills over the last twelve-month period. Then divide your energy costs for one year by twelve to arrive at your average monthly energy bill.

Compare this with the monthly bill of an "average" home or with the monthly payment plan amount quoted to you by your utility company. If your current bill is much greater, then there are probably many opportunities for improving the energy efficiency of your home. If your bills are lower than the average home, there may still be certain opportunities to make your home more energy efficient.

There are three key strategies to increase energy efficiency: air-sealing (leak-proofing) your home, adding insulation and efficient windows, and using more efficient appliances and equipment. Each is covered in part 3.

PART 3—Energy Efficiency

The average home in the United States wastes 30 to 50% of the energy it uses. If every home installed energy-efficient equipment and was well-insulated, individual homeowners and the national economy would reap tremendous savings. The following sections will help you identify where energy is being lost and how you can prevent future losses. Complete the assessment tables at the end of each section to see where improvements can be made.

Part 3a — Improving heating and cooling systems

The single greatest energy consumer in your home is the heating/cooling system (furnace, boiler, heat pump, wood stove, or air conditioner). This system has three parts: (1) heating/cooling unit(s), such as furnaces and air conditioners, (2) ducts or other distribution mechanism, and (3) a thermostat to control output. You can save energy in all three areas.

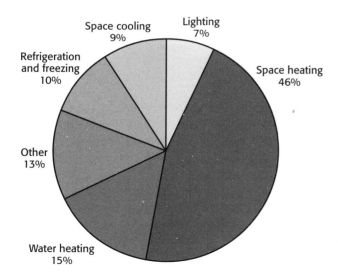

Figure 10.2 Typical distribution of residential energy use.
Data taken from U.S. Congress, Office of Technology Assessment, *Building Energy Efficiency*, OTA-E-518, 1992.

ARE YOUR ENERGY COSTS HIGH OR LOW?

Use the equations below to calculate and evaluate your energy consumption.

Total of heating/cooling bills for the past year (12 months)	$_____	
Divide by twelve to get average monthly bill (A)	÷ 12	
Average monthly bill	$_____	(A)
Average monthly bill for energy efficient houses similar to yours	$_____	(B)
(Note: Contact your local utility company for an estimate.)		

If A is larger than B, it may indicate that your home is using more energy — and costing more money — than it should. By increasing energy efficiency, you can cut your bills and save significant amounts of money over the long run.

How old are the parts of your system?

If your primary heating/cooling unit is over fifteen to twenty-five years old, it is probably not very energy efficient. Even if it still works, you may benefit by replacing it with a new energy-efficient model. A new device can pay for itself in fuel savings in only a few years. Or, if you find long-term financing for the new equipment, the dollar value of the monthly energy savings may exceed the monthly payment for the equipment, which would result in a positive cash flow.

Is your system getting proper maintenance?

All machines work more efficiently — and more safely — if they are inspected and maintained. Your furnace, air conditioner, and other heating/cooling equipment should be checked and serviced every year by a qualified professional. Monthly maintenance, such as inspecting and changing air filters, is recommended during the heating or cooling season. A forced-air system includes an air filter, which removes dust and debris before it reaches the air blower and heat-exchange coils. Dirt on the coils reduces efficiency, so you should change or clean your air filter on a regular basis.

Are you using your thermostat to save energy?

One of the easiest ways to save energy is to set thermostats at a lower temperature in winter and a higher temperature in summer so that the heating/cooling system runs less often. If a house is caulked and weather-stripped to prevent cold drafts, most people—when dressed appropriately—will be comfortable at 68 degrees Fahrenheit during winter. To save more energy, temperatures can be turned down to 50 or 60 degrees while you are sleeping or when the house is empty. During the summer, a thermostat setting of 72 degrees or higher is recommended. During times when the house is unoccupied, a summer thermostat setting of 80 to 85 degrees is recommended.

Digital or clock thermostats (also called automatic set-back thermostats) can be programmed to adjust the temperature in your house automatically (figure 10.3). For example, they can turn the heat down every night at 11 P.M. and bring the temperature back up by 6 A.M. before you get out of bed. The newest kind of residential thermostat, a home energy manager, allows many temperature settings throughout the week. Depending on your lifestyle, these set-back thermostats can pay for themselves in energy savings in as little as one or two years.

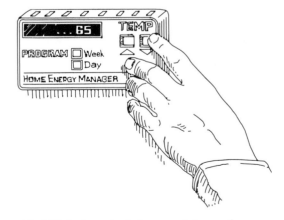

Figure 10.3 Digital or clock thermostats can be programmed to adjust the temperature automatically.

Is your distribution system working well?

Unless there is a heating/cooling unit in each room, you probably have a system to distribute hot or cool air from a central heater or air conditioner. Over 90% of central heating systems and virtually 100% of central residential cooling systems in America have forced-air distribution systems that use air ducts to move warm (or cold) air to the rooms of the house. If the duct system leaks, it can waste large amounts of energy.

Any ductwork located in an unheated space (such as an attic or crawl space) has a high potential for heat loss. Ducts in such spaces should be insulated. Also, all joints in the duct system, everywhere in the house, should be properly sealed to make sure all the warm or cool air gets where you want it to go.

Besides providing supply registers in each room to deliver heated/cooled air, there must be a return duct to allow air to get back to the heating/cooling unit. Many newer homes do not have a return register in every room, but rely on the space under a closed door to allow supply air to return to a centrally located return. If you have a room that is uncomfortable (hard to heat or cool) when the door is shut but is fine when the door is open, you probably have an air distribution problem. You can increase the cut under the door or call a heating and cooling specialist to resolve the problem.

The second most common heat distribution system uses hot water that is distributed through pipes to radiators or convectors. Pipes carrying hot water should be insulated everywhere—from boiler to radiator. Use a quality insulation material. Cheap materials degrade over time.

Assessment 3a — Improving heating/cooling systems

Use the table on the following page to identify areas where energy can be saved. Indicate your potential energy-loss level in the right-hand column. Although some choices may not correspond exactly to your situation, choose the response that best fits. Refer to the sections above if you need more information to complete the table.

Responding to your energy-loss potential

Your goal is to reduce the amount of energy that is wasted. Turn to the action checklist on page 105 to record the high and medium loss potentials you identified in the table. Use the recommendations in part 3a to help you identify ways to increase energy efficiency.

SAFETY NOTE

Your home receives outside air from all small holes and cracks in the structure, including any holes in the duct system that are located outside the conditioned space (such as an attic or crawl space).

Sealing a leaking duct system will reduce the amount of outside air that leaks into the home. While this will reduce energy consumption, you must also be aware of how it might affect combustion appliances and air quality within the home. The precautions listed under the "Safety Note" on page 102 apply here also. Duct sealing is a job best left to a professional.

Part 3b — Preventing loss of heated (or cooled) air

Once you have reached a comfortable temperature indoors, your aim is to keep it that way. Preventing unwanted air leaks and blocking heat transfer are two important approaches to making your home even more energy efficient.

Have you air-sealed your home?

Every house has openings through which outside air can enter. Some openings, such as open windows and doors, are obvious pathways for air entry. Others, such as cracks around window frames, are unintended pathways for leaks (figure 10.4). This uncontrolled leakage of air, known as infiltration, can account for a

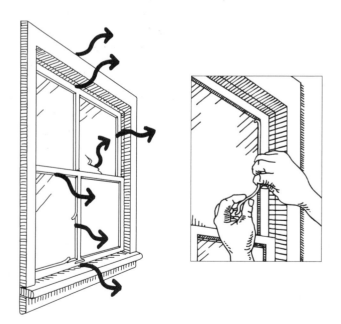

Figure 10.4 Air leakage is often the primary cause of heat loss from windows and doors. Seal leaks with caulking and weatherstripping.

	LOW ENERGY LOSS	MEDIUM ENERGY LOSS	HIGH ENERGY LOSS	YOUR LOSS POTENTIAL
Age of heating/ cooling equipment	Equipment is less than five years old.	Equipment is five to fifteen years old.	Equipment is older than fifteen years.	❑ Low ❑ Medium ❑ High
Maintenance of heating/ cooling equipment	Air filters are changed every month during use, and equipment is serviced at least every two years.	Filters are changed occasionally, and the system is maintained on an irregular basis.	Filters are not changed or rarely changed, and the system is not maintained.	❑ Low ❑ Medium ❑ High
Air-temperature thermostat	A modern thermostat with variable temperature set-back is installed. It is routinely used to minimize energy consumption.	A newer thermostat is installed, but it is not used to regulate temperatures at night or when the house is empty.	An older thermostat is in use. It is set to maintain a constant temperature.	❑ Low ❑ Medium ❑ High
Duct location	All duct work is located in heated/cooled space.	Some duct work is located in unheated space.	All duct work is located in unheated space.	❑ Low ❑ Medium ❑ High
Ductwork in unheated space (if applicable)	All ductwork in unheated space is insulated.	Some ductwork in unheated space is insulated.	There is no insulation on ducts.	❑ Low ❑ Medium ❑ High
Return duct	There are air-return ducts in every room, or bedroom doors are left open.	There is one "central" air return. Bedroom doors are shut at night but there is a 2-inch or greater space under the doors.	There is one "central" air return. Bedroom doors are shut at night, and there is little space between the bottom of the doors and the floor.	❑ Low ❑ Medium ❑ High
Air-sealing ducts and registers	Seams in the duct system are caulked or sealed, especially where air registers enter rooms.	There are no visible gaps in the duct system.	Gaps are visible in the duct system or around room air registers.	❑ Low ❑ Medium ❑ High
Air intake or air handler	The intake/handler is located in heated space.	The intake/handler is located in unheated space (for example, a crawl space or attic).	The air intake/handler is located in a garage.*	❑ Low ❑ Medium ❑ High

* **SAFETY NOTE:** If your air handler is in your garage, NEVER leave your car running in the garage. The air handler can pick up car exhaust fumes and distribute them to the house through the duct system.

large portion of the total heat loss in a home—typically about 30% of the total heating bill. Cold (or warm) air entering a home must be heated (or cooled) if the home is to remain comfortable.

Sealing your home against air leakage is not difficult, but it does require detailed information to be done right. For details on how to reduce air leaks, contact your local Cooperative Extension office or the U.S. Department of Energy's Energy Efficiency and Renewable Energy Clearinghouse (EREC). (See "For More Information" on page 104.)

Does your home need more insulation?

Even if you air-seal your house, you still need to prevent the transfer of heat or cold air through walls, floors, or ceilings. Insulation acts like a blanket to retain the heat or cool air your system produces. Insulation materials are assigned an *R-value,* which is a measure of how well they *Resist* the flow of heat energy into or out of your home. The larger the R-value, the more heat (or cool air) is kept where you want it.

The recommended amount of insulation for a home varies with geographic location. If you have extreme temperatures in your area, you will need more insulation. Your local building supplier should be able to provide you with good recommendations. The EREC publication "Insulation Materials and Strategies" describes various insulation products available and provides insulation recommendations for all areas of the United States by zip code. It also helps you decide if you should attempt the job yourself or have it done professionally. (See "For More Information" on page 104 for information on how to contact EREC.)

Assessment 3b — Preventing loss of heated (or cooled) air

As before, indicate your potential energy-loss level in the right-hand column in the table on the following page. Although some choices may not correspond exactly to your situation, choose the response that best fits. Refer to the sections above if you need more information to complete the table.

Responding to your energy-loss potential

Your goal is to reduce the amount of energy you use. On the action checklist (see page 105), record the high and medium loss potentials you identified above. Use the recommendations in part 3b to help you find ways to increase energy efficiency.

Part 3c — Increasing efficiency of domestic hot water systems

After heating and cooling your home, heating water for domestic consumption is the next largest energy

---

SAFETY NOTE

Proceed with caution. As stated before, *your home must be a healthy place to live.* Air-sealing may save energy, but it can also trap deadly pollutants. Air-sealing can cause a dangerous situation by reducing the air available for combustion appliances. Do not attempt to air-seal your home until you have taken care of these problem areas:

- Unvented gas or kerosene heaters or unvented gas fireplaces/logs must be removed or vented outdoors.

- If you have a gas cook stove that is not vented to the outside by a power-vented hood, do not extensively air-seal your home. Alternatively, open a kitchen window ¼ inch while cooking and run an exhaust fan.

- If you have a high level of radon in your home, properly air-sealing can help reduce the problem. However, you should monitor radon levels carefully and contact a professional if the problem is not fixed. (See chapter 9, "Indoor Air Quality," for more information about radon.)

- If you have natural-draft appliances, do not extensively air-seal your home without seeking the advice of an energy services professional.

---

user. There are several ways to reduce the amount of energy you use to heat water.

The simplest thing you can do to save energy used for water heating is to turn down the water heater temperature. Each 10-degree reduction in water heater temperature will save you 3 to 5% on your annual water heating bill. Lowering the water temperature will also increase the lifetime of your water heater and reduce the risk of someone being burned by the hot water. Children and the elderly are most at risk of being scalded from water that is too hot.

Most water heaters are factory set around 140 degrees Fahrenheit. For most household uses, that is higher than necessary. Usually, 120-degree water is adequate unless you have an automatic dishwasher without a temperature booster. In this case, you may need to keep the temperature set at 140 degrees for optimal dishwashing performance.

Wrapping your water heater with insulation can reduce water heating energy use by 4 to 9%. Except for some new water heaters that come with high levels of foam insulation and do not need any more, the addition of insulation usually pays for itself in less than one year. Water heater insulation blankets are widely available at hardware stores and come in standard sizes to fit 40-, 60-, and 80-gallon water heaters. Be sure to follow the manufacturer's instructions for installation.

Reducing hot water consumption will reduce the amount of energy needed. Fix any leaking pipes and consider installing low-flow shower heads. Washing laundry in cold rather than hot water will also save energy.

Hot water pipes should be insulated wherever they are accessible. Either preformed foam insulation or wraparound fiberglass insulation can be used.

Assessment 3c — Increasing efficiency of domestic hot water systems
In the table on the following page, indicate your potential energy-loss level in the right-hand column. Refer to the sections above if you need more information to complete the table.

Responding to your energy-loss potential
Your goal is to reduce the amount of energy you use. On the action checklist (see page 105), record the high and medium loss potentials you identified above. Use the recommendations in part 3c to help you find ways to increase energy efficiency.

▶ ASSESSMENT 3b — Preventing Loss of Heated (or Cooled) Air

	LOW ENERGY LOSS	MEDIUM ENERGY LOSS	HIGH ENERGY LOSS	YOUR LOSS POTENTIAL
Attic	All potential leak points are sealed or weather-stripped.	Only some potential leak points are sealed.	Most potential leak points are not sealed.	❏ Low ❏ Medium ❏ High
Windows and doors	All windows and doors are sealed with caulk and weather-stripping and tested for leaks. Newer, well-sealed, double-paned windows are installed.	Only some windows and doors are caulked and weather-stripped. Older or leaky storm windows are used. Some windows are sealed in winter with plastic sheets.	Windows are older and not sealed. Storm windows may be absent.	❏ Low ❏ Medium ❏ High
Basement or crawl space	Sill plates, service entrances, windows, and wall cracks are sealed with caulk or foam.	Leaks have been detected but are not fully sealed.	No sealing has been attempted.	❏ Low ❏ Medium ❏ High
Attic insulation	Insulation is equal to or greater than levels recommended for my region.		Insulation is well below the recommended levels—OR—attic is not insulated.	❏ Low ❏ High
Insulation in walls (above-ground)	Wall cavities are insulated with loose fill or 3-inch to 5-inch batt.		There is no insulation in wall cavities.	❏ Low ❏ High
Insulation in walls (heated basements)	Walls are insulated with rigid foam or batt, according to the regional recommendations.		Walls are not insulated.	❏ Low ❏ High

	LOW ENERGY LOSS	MEDIUM ENERGY LOSS	HIGH ENERGY LOSS	YOUR LOSS POTENTIAL
Thermostat setting	Thermostat is set at 120°F.	Thermostat is set at 130°F.	Thermostat is set at 140°F or higher.	❐ Low ❐ Medium ❐ High
Insulation	A new, highly insulated water heater or water heater blanket is installed.		An older water heater with no added blanket is in use.	❐ Low ❐ High
Water conservation	Low-flow shower heads are installed, and there are no leaking faucets. A conscious effort is made to conserve hot water.	There are no leaking faucets. Some effort is made to minimize hot water use.	There are leaking faucets, and no low-flow fixtures are installed.	❐ Low ❐ Medium ❐ High
Pipe insulation	All accessible hot water pipes are insulated.	Some accessible hot water pipes are insulated.	There is no pipe insulation.	❐ Low ❐ Medium ❐ High

ACTION CHECKLIST

Go back over the assessment tables and make sure that you have recorded all high and medium risks and energy-loss potentials. Next, list the improvements you plan to make. You can use recommendations from this chapter or from other sources to help you pick actions you are likely to take. Write down a date to keep you on schedule. You don't have to do everything at once, but try to eliminate the most serious problems as soon as you can. Often it helps to tackle the inexpensive actions first.

For More Information

Energy Efficiency and Renewable Energy Clearinghouse (EREC)

The U.S. Department of Energy provides energy information through the Energy Efficiency and Renewable Energy Clearinghouse (EREC). EREC will send detailed information on the topics in this assessment, and much more. Call them toll-free at (800) DOE-EREC/(800)-363-3732, Monday–Friday, 9A.M.–7P.M., eastern standard time.

American Council for an Energy Efficient Economy

The American Council for an Energy Efficient Economy can provide information on energy-efficient appliances. Contact them at 2140 Shattuck Avenue, Suite 202, Berkeley, CA 94704; (510) 549-9914. Ask for a current list of publications.

Publications

Heede, Richard. *Homemade Money: How to Save Energy and Dollars in Your Home.* Amherst, New Hampshire: Brick House Publishing, 1995. This publication is 260 pages long and is available for $14.95 per copy from the Rocky Mountain Institute, 1739 Snowmass Creek Road, Snowmass, CO 81654-9199.

Nisson, Ned and Alex Wilson. *The Virginia Energy Savers Handbook: A Guide to Saving Energy, Money, and the Environment.* Virginia Department of Mines, Minerals, and Energy, 1993. This 120-page guide is available from the Virginia Department of Mines, Minerals, and Energy, Division of Energy, 202 North Ninth Street, 8th Floor, Richmond, VA 23219; (804) 692-3218.

Home*A*Syst Helps Ensure Your Safety

This *Home*A*Syst* handbook covers a variety of topics to help homeowners examine and address their most important environmental concerns. See the complete list of chapters in the table of contents at the beginning of this handbook. For more information about topics covered in *Home*A*Syst*, or for information

Heating and Cooling Systems:
Saving Energy and Keeping Safe

Write all high and medium risks and energy loss potentials below.	What can you do to reduce the risk or energy loss potential?	Set a target date for action.
Sample: Water heater is not insulated.	Buy a ready-made insulation blanket at the hardware store.	One week from today: March 8

about laws and regulations specific to your area, contact your nearest Cooperative Extension office.

Contact the National Farm*A*Syst/Home*A*Syst Office at: B142 Steenbock Library, 550 Babcock Drive, Madison, WI 53706-1293; phone: (608) 262-0024; e-mail: <HOMEASYST@MACC.WISC.EDU>.

Figures 10.1, 10.3, and 10.4 were adapted from Ned Nisson and Alex Wilson, *The Virginia Energy Savers Handbook: A Guide to Saving Energy, Money, and the Environment*, 1993.

This chapter was written by Lori S. Marsh, Associate Professor and Extension Engineer, Department of Biological Systems Engineering, Virginia Polytechnic Institute and State University.

Chapter 11

MANAGING HOUSEHOLD WASTE: Preventing, Reusing, Recycling, and Composting

by Shirley Niemeyer, University of Nebraska–Lincoln; Michael P. Vogel, Montana State University Extension Service; and Kathleen Parrott, Virginia Polytechnic Institute and State University

There are many ways to reduce household waste and many alternatives for disposing of the waste you do make. This chapter will help you examine your current waste disposal and consumption practices and how they may affect air, soil, and water quality on your property or in your home or community. It covers:

1. *Preventing and Minimizing Waste* — choosing products and services to reduce waste ("precycling" or "enviro-shopping")

2. *Reusing, Recycling, and Composting* — creative ways to deal with wastes

3. *Waste Disposal on Your Property* — alternatives to on-site dumping and burning

Why should you be concerned?

As the U.S. population increases, the amount of waste produced each year also rises. In fact, material consumption has increased faster than the population. Studies estimate that in 1994, each person produced around 4.4 pounds of waste each day—a significant increase from the 2.7 pounds produced per person daily in 1960.

Surveys also found that most consumers do not realize what comprises solid waste. Many, for example, think that we throw away more plastics by weight than we really do, or that disposable diapers are a major problem (they aren't). Figure 11.1 shows what is in the mountain of solid waste thrown away in the United States each year. What would you find if you examined wastes from *your* household over a year's time?

What is the big picture?

The United States is number one in waste produced, energy consumed, and use of the earth's natural resources. While the United States has only 6% of the

world's population, it uses about 40 to 50% of the world's nonrenewable resources and produces an estimated 15 to 38% of the world's waste. We use more than our share of the world's natural resources and often turn them into waste or unusable products. Changing from a resource-consuming lifestyle to a resource-conserving one would help maintain natural resources and create less waste.

The problem with waste

Most of our waste is destined for landfills. But because of public concern about landfill location and stricter disposal regulations in many parts of the country, acceptable landfill space is becoming scarcer and/or more expensive. Environmental laws have forced many dumps and incinerators to close or modernize at a cost of millions of dollars. In areas without

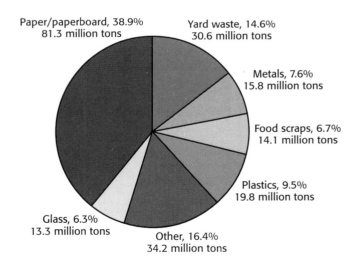

Figure 11.1 What is in our solid waste?
Source: Franklin Associates, Ltd. Source and Characterization of Municipal Solid Waste in the United States: 1995 Update. U.S. Environmental Protection Agency, 1996.

nearby disposal options, consumers may be paying higher rates to have waste hauled hundreds of miles to be buried or incinerated. As a result, waste has become a major environmental and economic issue for consumers and municipalities.

The good news is that these problems have caused us to look for new ways to deal with or reduce our waste. Producing less waste and finding creative alternatives for dealing with waste not only saves taxpayer dollars but helps protect air, soil, and water quality and the health of people and wildlife.

PART 1 — Preventing and Minimizing Waste

If you don't produce waste, you won't need to get rid of it — it's that simple. But since we all generate at least some waste, we need to think about ways to make less.

A strategy to help maintain natural resources and create less waste is *source reduction,* which is defined by the U.S. Environmental Protection Agency as "reducing the amount of materials entering the waste stream by redesigning products or patterns of production or consumption." An example of source reduction is using returnable beverage containers.

Part 1 will help you examine your potential for cutting the amount of waste you produce and preventing some kinds waste completely. At the end of part 1, fill out the assessment table to determine your *waste potential.* Use the information below to help answer the questions.

Can you become a waste-conscious shopper?

You make purchasing decisions every day, and each purchase involves a certain amount of waste production and use of natural resources. Whether buying groceries, toys, furniture, or appliances, your decision to select a certain product or no product at all will determine the type and volume of waste that you must someday discard. If you buy with the environment in mind — that is, if you use your purchasing power to minimize your impact on the environment — you will select products that produce a minimum of waste, last longer, and use less natural resources. "Precycling" and "enviro-shopping" are terms that refer to this kind of purchasing. An "enviro-shopper" typically asks the following questions before making a purchase.

How much do I need?

Among other things, enviro-shopping means buying only what you need. A good price or bulk packaging may tempt you to buy more paint, food, or household cleaner than you really need. But what may seem like a "good deal" may end up wasting money and natural resources, because the unused or spoiled product will eventually have to be thrown away. Make sure you can use what you buy, or find someone who can use your leftovers.

Are my purchases long-lasting and reusable?

In our "throw-away" society, it is sometimes hard to find good-quality products at an affordable price. Although durable products may be more expensive, they are usually a better investment in the long run. Look for products that can be fixed when broken. Long-lasting products make good hand-me-downs, too.

Products and materials that can be reused—passed along to someone else or used for other purposes—save money and conserve resources. For example, reusable gift bags can reduce your need to buy wrapping paper. If it is safe to do so, carry your own shopping bag or use no bag at all. In a world with increasing numbers of disposable and single-use products, it is a real challenge to avoid waste when shopping.

Is the product package recyclable?

Many product containers and packaging materials are potentially recyclable — such as glass bottles, paper, plastic bags, and cardboard boxes. To promote recycling, many manufacturers use a chasing-arrows recycling symbol (figure 11.2). But be careful; this symbol may mean the product or packaging is made from materials that are *suitable* for recycling *if* your local recycling program will take them. If a product cannot be recycled locally, then the product packaging is *not* truly recyclable—at least not where you live. The list of materials that your local recycling program will accept probably changes over time, so you will need to keep up-to-date.

If you can't recycle something locally, you might be able to take it to a close neighboring community that will accept it. But don't waste more natural resources (such as gasoline) than you will save by recycling. Combine trips to recycling facilities with other tasks.

Is the product or its packaging made from recycled materials?

There is a surprising variety of products made from recycled material: everything from carpets to detergent bottles. Once materials are recycled, they will be made into new products or packaging *only if* there is a market for them. As a consumer, you can use your buying power to support and encourage markets for recycled-material products. "Closing the loop"—that is, recycling *and* buying recycled—ensures that materials are cycled again and again.

On product packaging, look for the words "made from recycled materials" or, even better, "made from *post-consumer* recycled materials." *Post-consumer* means that all or part of the packaging is made from materials that have been recycled by consumers in community recycling programs; the packaging has been in the consumer's hands before. Each year, for example, billions of recycled aluminum beverage cans are

Figure 11.2 The recycling symbol means the product or packaging is recyclable. But if your local recycling program won't accept the product, it isn't really recyclable — at least not where you live.

> ## HOW MUCH HOUSEHOLD WASTE DO YOU MAKE EACH DAY?
>
> This project is for the truly adventurous. Carry a large bag for one to three days and put all of your daily waste inside (if it is safe to carry). Don't change your buying or eating habits. You might want to keep wet wastes in plastic bags so things don't get too messy.
>
> At the end of the experiment, weigh the bag. If you carried your bag for three days, divide the total weight by three to get the average daily amount of waste. Then analyze your waste: How much of the total weight or volume is paper? How much is recyclable, and how much is potentially hazardous? How much could have been avoided? How many pounds of waste would you produce in a *year*?

melted down and made into new cans. But remember—just because you see a chasing arrow, don't assume that the product or packaging can be locally recycled.

Do I buy products with the least amount of packaging?

About a third of the paper, plastic, glass, cardboard, and metal we throw away comes from packaging. While packaging serves many useful purposes — such as preventing food spoilage, ensuring customer safety, meeting legal requirements, and providing information — some is unnecessary, wastes natural resources, and soon after purchase ends up as waste.

Good enviro-shopping means choosing products that have the least amount of wrapping (as long as your safety is assured). Buying bulk foods (if they won't be wasted) and selecting concentrated products are examples of minimizing waste from packaging (figure 11.3). If your packaging selections are limited, tell the store manager what you want, or write or call the product manufacturer about your community's solid waste situation and your preference for minimally packaged products.

Assessment 1 — Preventing and minimizing waste

Use the table on the following page to identify areas where you can minimize waste. Indicate your waste potential in the right-hand column. Although some choices may not correspond exactly to your situation, choose the response that best fits. Refer to the information above to help you answer the questions.

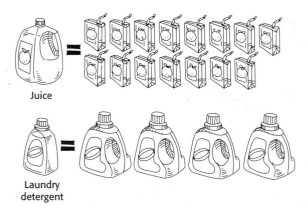

Juice

Laundry detergent

Figure 11.3 Selecting concentrated products is one way to minimize waste from packaging.

Responding to your waste potential

Your goal is to reduce the amount of waste you produce — especially waste that ends up in a landfill or incinerator. Turn to the action checklist on page 115 to record the high and medium waste potentials you identified in the assessment table. Use the ideas in part 1 to help you become an enviro-shopper.

PART 2 — Reusing, Recycling, and Composting

Once you make waste, it has to go somewhere. Part 2 reviews three ways to keep materials *out* of a landfill or incinerator. For each item of waste, there are three questions to ask:

First, is it reusable?

Reuse should be your first objective, as it typically has the least environmental impact. Refillable glass beverage bottles are an example of a reusable product. Empty bottles are collected and trucked back to the bottler, where they are washed and refilled. Natural resources are still used in cleaning and hauling the product for reuse. To compare this to recycling, see the story about glass recycling in the next section.

Often, reuse is limited only by the imagination—you can usually find uses for more materials than you realize. Sharing old clothes and used furniture is a common form of reuse. If you can't share with friends or family, try to donate usable items to programs like Goodwill or thrift shops. Holding a neighborhood yard sale is a good way to eliminate unwanted possessions. Give your packaging foam "peanuts" to a local gift shop, or see if neighbors can use your excess paint, lumber, or empty plastic pails—if the items can be reused safely. Try listing materials you want to get rid of on a postcard and posting the card on a local community bulletin board. Reusing an item is a great way to save natural resources if recycling is not available and if it does not use more natural resources than other options.

Second, is it recyclable?

Studies have shown that more than half of all household wastes are recyclable. Recycling is a good idea,

▶ **ASSESSMENT 1 —Preventing and Minimizing Waste**

	LOW WASTE POTENTIAL	MEDIUM WASTE POTENTIAL	HIGH WASTE POTENTIAL	YOUR WASTE POTENTIAL
Quantities purchased	I only buy what I need and avoid accumulating unused products.	I sometimes buy more product than I can use.	I often buy more product than I can use.	❑ Low ❑ Medium ❑ High
Product durability and potential for reuse	I select products based on their durability, ease of repair, and potential for reuse.	I sometimes consider durability, ease of repair, or potential for reuse.	I never consider durability, ease of repair, or potential for reuse.	❑ Low ❑ Medium ❑ High
Recyclability of packaging	I regularly purchase containers/packaging that can be recycled locally.	I sometimes consider recyclability when making purchases.	I never consider recyclability.	❑ Low ❑ Medium ❑ High
Packaging selected	When safe to do so, I select packaging that minimizes waste.	I sometimes consider packaging that minimizes waste.	I never consider packaging that minimizes waste.	❑ Low ❑ Medium ❑ High

although it still requires energy and other resources and produces waste and pollution. For empty glass bottles to be recycled into new bottles, for example, they must be collected, sorted, sometimes crushed, and trucked to a glass factory where they are washed, melted, and re-formed into new bottles. The new bottles are then trucked to a beverage company to be filled. In the end, though, recycling usually does save more resources and result in less pollution than making items from raw natural resources.

Check with your local or area recycling business to see what is recycled in your area, where items are recycled, and how to prepare items for recycling (figure 11.4). Remember to keep current about what your local program will accept; use the table below to keep track. Plastic milk jugs, for example, are usually recyclable, but wax-coated paper milk cartons can be recycled only in a few areas.

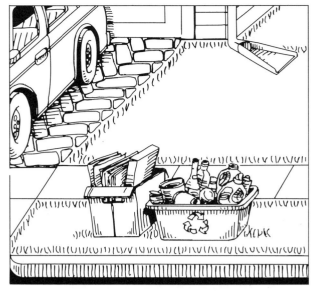

Figure 11.4 Find out what is recyclable in your area and how to prepare items for recycling.

WHAT CAN YOU RECYCLE IN YOUR AREA?

Item	Recycled where?	How should it be prepared?
Paper/cardboard		
Glass		
Plastic		
Aluminum		
Steel		
Other metals		
Automobile batteries		
Oil		
Tires		
White goods/appliances		
Wood/lumber		
Bricks/concrete		
Other:		

A growing number of programs require recycling by law. You should not limit recycling to typical grocery store purchases such as aluminum cans, cardboard, glass bottles, and plastic milk jugs. There may be local scrap dealers or industrial salvage yards that want your broken appliances, used vehicles, wood and metal wastes, bricks, concrete, doors, windows, and so on. Many localities and/or states now require residents to recycle large appliances, car batteries, used motor oil, and other recoverable materials.

Third, can it be composted?

Yard trimmings and food wastes typically make up 10 to 25% of the wastes going into landfills. Your amount of yard and food wastes depends on your eating and gardening habits, yard size, climate, and region. Many landfills across the country have banned yard waste from disposal because of its large volume, high moisture content, and potential to contribute to landfill gas and groundwater problems. Composting—or "nature's recycling"—is a much more effective way to handle organic waste.

Composting is a natural process that turns kitchen and garden wastes (with the help of microbes, earthworms, and fungi) into a high-quality soil conditioner. Many common materials can be composted in your own backyard: leaves, grass clippings, plant trimmings, straw, some kitchen scraps (but not animal wastes like fat, bones, or pet manure), and even small amounts of paper. The final product is a dark brown, crumbly compost that has a clean, earthy scent. It can be spread on lawns or mixed with garden soil as an excellent natural soil conditioner. As an alternative to landfill disposal, many communities have established yard waste compost programs with convenient drop-off sites or curbside pick-up. To compost at home, you can use one of the many compact and efficient composting bins on the market, or you can build your own (see figure 11.5 for examples). For kitchen scraps, you might even try a type of indoor composting that uses worms to break down wastes. Your nearest Cooperative Extension office can provide you with more detailed information about composting.

Assessment 2 — Reusing, recycling, and composting

Use the table below to identify preferred methods to keep waste out of the landfill. Indicate your waste-potential level in the right-hand column. Although some choices may not correspond exactly to your situation, choose the response that best fits. Refer to the information above to help you answer the questions.

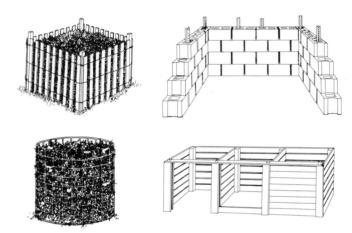

Figure 11.5 Examples of compost bins made with snow fence, concrete blocks, wire mesh, and pressure-treated wood.

▶ ASSESSMENT 2 —Reusing, Recycling, and Composting

	LOW WASTE POTENTIAL	MEDIUM WASTE POTENTIAL	HIGH WASTE POTENTIAL	YOUR WASTE POTENTIAL
Reusing	I reuse as many household wastes as possible.	I reuse items when it is convenient to do so.	I never reuse items.	❏ Low ❏ Medium ❏ High
Recycling	I recycle as many household wastes as possible.	I recycle when it is convenient to do so.	I never recycle.	❏ Low ❏ Medium ❏ High
Composting	I compost all yard wastes and kitchen vegetable scraps at home or in a city program.	I compost some yard or kitchen wastes.	I never compost.	❏ Low ❏ Medium ❏ High

Responding to your waste potential

Your goal is to reduce waste or find the best alternatives for dealing with it. Turn to the action checklist on page 115 to record the high and medium waste potentials you identified above. The information in part 2 can help you plan improvements.

PART 3 — Waste Disposal on Your Property

Disposing of household waste by burning it or dumping it on private property can pose threats to your health and the environment. Although these disposal methods have been used in many rural areas for decades, local and state laws are becoming more restrictive. Most states ban illegal dumping or burning of waste to protect soil, water, and air quality. Complete the table at the end of this section to determine your risks, and consider alternatives to on-site methods of disposal.

Do you burn household waste?

Some residents use burn barrels to get rid of many household wastes. When paper, plastics, printing inks, batteries, and other common materials are burned, a noxious mix of chemicals can be released into the air (see sidebar at right). Some of these—such as lead or mercury or even byproducts given off when leaves are burned—can be hazardous to breathe.

Eventually, most byproducts from burning are removed from the air by rain or snow and are deposited on land or in water. Due to concerns about such depositing of hazardous air pollutants, most states and localities have passed laws to restrict if or what you can burn. In most areas, especially urban and suburban settings, open burning has been banned.

The ash residue from burning also contains hazards — including heavy metals and other toxic substances. If this ash is dumped on your property, it can contaminate soil and water. To find out about burning restrictions that apply in your area, check with your local law enforcement agency or the fire or health department. The ash may have to be taken to a licensed landfill.

Do you dump household waste on your land?

Waste dumped on your property is not only unsightly, it may contain harmful chemicals that can leach out and contaminate groundwater (figure 11.6), or be spread by wind and rain. Discarded paint, for example, may contain lead or mercury. If not properly rinsed, pesticide containers may contain toxic residue, and used oil filters usually harbor petroleum prod-

---

ucts and harmful metals. These pollutants can soak into the soil, pollute well water, and find their way into nearby lakes, streams, or wetlands. If your waste contains hazardous substances—even in small quantities—it can cause problems. Another problem is caused by discarded tires, which provide a haven for mosquitoes.

Real estate disclosure laws in some states or areas require property owners to disclose environmental information such as known dumpsites or other hazards on the property being sold. So if you have a dump or burn site, such as an oil or pesticide dump site, you may be required to tell potential buyers.

For more information about disposing of waste on your property, contact your local or state health department, state department of natural resources or environmental quality, or a licensed landfill operator.

Do you dump household waste down a storm sewer or drain?

Especially for homes served by street drains and storm sewers, any solid or liquid wastes exposed to the weather—including pet wastes, motor oil spills, solvent spills, solvent-based paints and products, and other product spills—can wash directly into lakes and streams. Storm sewers, remember, are rarely connected to wastewater treatment facilities.

Some materials, like foam "peanuts" and other plastic debris, can be transported by storm runoff to open water where they may be mistaken for food and eaten by fish or birds.

Dumping potentially hazardous substances down a drain that leads to a septic system or sewer system can also cause problems; see chapter 4, "Household Wastewater," and chapter 5, "Managing Hazardous Household Products," for more information.

Assessment 3 — Waste disposal on your property

The assessment table on the following page can help you examine potential risks due to on-site waste dis-

posal. Choose the statement in the right-hand column that best fits your situation. Refer to the information above in part 3 to help you respond.

WHICH WASTES ARE HAZARDOUS?

By reading product labels, you can generally tell which ones have hazardous ingredients. Look for words like DANGER, FLAMMABLE, POISON, VAPOR HARMFUL, or FATAL IF SWALLOWED. These are clues that a substance in the product is potentially hazardous to your health.

Carefully dispose of such products—especially if unused portions of the product are in liquid form. Although dry chemicals can be hazardous, liquids can more easily injure waste haulers, react with other discarded chemicals to start fires or create deadly gases, or seep through soils and into water sources. The best approach for dealing with these products is to use them up, if it is safe and legal to do so, so nothing is left to discard.

Always read the label for disposal recommendations, or contact the manufacturer. For more information on dealing with hazardous wastes, see chapter 5, "Managing Hazardous Household Products."

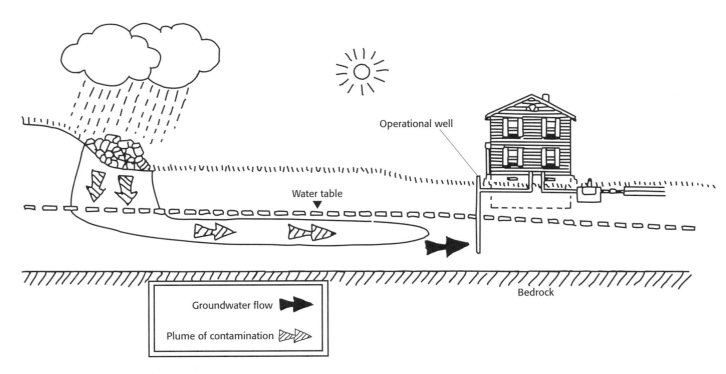

Figure 11.6 Waste dumped on or near your property may contain harmful chemicals that can leach out and contaminate groundwater.

	LOW RISK	MEDIUM RISK	HIGH RISK	YOUR RISK
Burning waste	No household waste is burned on-site.	Only non-toxic materials are burned. If burning is legal, burning guidelines are strictly followed.	Mixtures of waste (including paper, solvents, batteries, and plastics) are burned, releasing metals, acids, and chlorine compounds.	❏ Low ❏ Medium ❏ High
On-site dumping	No household waste is dumped on my property or on public property.	Only non-toxic wastes are dumped on-site — in an approved, properly designed site.	Household wastes and liquids, appliances, tires, and other junk are dumped on-site.	❏ Low ❏ Medium ❏ High
Dumping down storm sewers or drains	No hazardous materials are discarded in a sewer system, septic system, or storm drain.	Some runoff from a driveway carries spills and yard chemicals away; runoff occasionally flows into storm sewers.	Hazardous and other wastes are improperly discarded in a sewer system, septic system, or storm drain.	❏ Low ❏ Medium ❏ High

Responding to risks

Your goal is to reduce your risks. On the action checklist on the following page, write all high and medium risks you identified. Use the ideas in part 3 to help plan actions to take.

ACTION CHECKLIST

Go back over the assessment tables to ensure that all medium and high waste potentials and risks you identified are listed in the action checklist on the following page. For each item listed, write down the improvements you plan to make. Use recommendations from this chapter and other resources to decide on actions you are likely to complete. A target date will keep you on schedule. You don't have to do everything at once, but try to eliminate the most serious problems as soon as you can. Often it helps to tackle the inexpensive actions first.

For More Information

Recycling, composting, and waste disposal

Contact your local health or sanitation department, recycling center, fire department, city office, or Cooperative Extension office. Get the latest list of what is recyclable and how to prepare items for recycling. Ask for information on composting and other disposal alternatives and a schedule of hazardous waste collection days. Find out where to take used motor oil, batteries, and appliances.

Local regulations on burning and dumping

If you are unsure of dumping and burning laws in your area, contact your state or local health or environmental agency. In most states, it is illegal or requires permits.

Publications

Franklin Associates, Ltd. *Characterization of Municipal Solid Waste in the United States: 1995 Update.* Report no. 530/R96/001. U.S. Environmental Protection Agency. Copies are available from the National Center for Environmental Publications and Information, PO Box 42419, Cincinnati, OH 45242-2419.

Lund, Herbert F., ed. *The McGraw-Hill Recycling Handbook.* New York: McGraw-Hill, Inc. 1993.

Makower, Joel. *The Green Consumer Supermarket Guide.* New York: Penguin Books. 1991.

Rathje, William and Cullen Murphy. *Rubbish! The Archaeology of Garbage.* New York: Harper Collins. 1992.

Sax, N. Irving and Richard J. Lewis. *Hawley's Condensed Chemical Dictionary.* New York: Van Ostrand Reinhold. 1987.

Tchobanoglous, G., H. Theisen, and S. Vigil. *Integrated Solid Waste Management: Engineering Principles and Management Issues.* New York: McGraw-Hill, Inc. 1993.

Wackernagel, Mathis and William E. Rees. *Our Ecological Footprint: Reducing Human Impact on the Earth.* Philadelphia: New Society Publishers. 1996.

Managing Household Waste:
Preventing, Reusing, Recycling, and Composting

Write all high and medium waste-making potentials and risks below.	What can you do to cut waste or reduce the risk?	Set a target date for action.
Sample: Products are purchased without considering whether the packaging is recyclable.	Find out about town recycling program and try to buy products with packaging that can be recycled locally.	One week from today: March 8

*Home*A*Syst* Helps Ensure Your Safety

This *Home*A*Syst* handbook covers a variety of topics to help homeowners examine and address their most important environmental concerns. See the complete list of chapters in the table of contents at the beginning of this handbook. For more information about topics covered in *Home*A*Syst,* or for information about laws and regulations specific to your area, contact your nearest Cooperative Extension office.

Contact the National Farm*A*Syst/Home*A*Syst Office at: B142 Steenbock Library, 550 Babcock Drive, Madison, WI 53706-1293; phone: (608) 262-0024; e-mail: <HOMEASYST@MACC.WISC.EDU>.

This chapter was written by Shirley Niemeyer, Professor and Extension Specialist, Environment of the Home/Housing, University of Nebraska–Lincoln; Michael P. Vogel, Professor and Extension Housing Specialist, Montana State University Extension Service; and Kathleen Parrott, Associate Professor and Extension Housing Specialist, Virginia Polytechnic Institute and State University.

Other Publications from NRAES

Burning Wood and Coal, NRAES-23
Whether you are a veteran user of solid fuels or a novice, this manual tells you all you need to know about wood and coal for home heating. Eight chapters are included — The Solid Fuels: Evaluating Your Options, Fireplaces, Stoves, Furnaces and Boilers, Installation, Chimneys, Wood as a Fuel, and Coal as a Fuel. An appendix about cutting firewood with a chainsaw is included as well. (1985) *90 pages*

Composting to Reduce the Waste Stream: A Guide to Small Scale Food and Yard Waste Composting, NRAES-43
Composting transforms organic waste into a soil-enhancing material. This publication covers the composting process, composting methods and alternatives, making and maintaining a compost pile, and using compost. Seventeen figures, six tables, and plans for constructing nine different types of compost bins are included as well. This guide is intended for home composters or those involved in educational programs to promote home composting. (1991) *44 pages*

Home and Yard Improvements Handbook, MWPS-21
A complete do-it-yourself guide to home improvement. Easy-to-follow instructions show how to add storage and recreational areas; build closets, kitchen cabinets, a garage, or a deck; repair a damp basement; or add attic storage. A special section about adapting a home for wheelchair access is included as well. Ninety-one figures and twenty-two tables supplement the text. (1978) *100 pages*

Home Buyers' Guide: Financing and Evaluating Prospective Homes, NRAES-50
This publication explores the home-buying process. Six major areas are covered—getting information and assistance, financing a home, choosing a location, evaluating a floor plan, inspecting a home, and assessing environmental safety. This guide was designed for adult education classes, individuals planning to buy a home, and professionals who offer advice to prospective home buyers. (1991) *72 pages*

Home Water Treatment, NRAES-48
This guide will help homeowners decide if water treatment is necessary and, if it is, which treatment device is appropriate for a particular problem. Homeowners on a public water system may find the information useful for improving the taste, smell, or appearance of their water or for treating contaminants that may leach from household plumbing. Appendixes cover U.S. Environmental Protection Agency drinking water contaminants and potential treatment devices or methods for their removal. Also included are forty-one illustrations, thirty tables, a glossary, and a list of references. (1995) *120 pages*

House Planning Handbook, MWPS-16
Whether you plan to buy, rent, or build a house, this handbook will help you select a functional and satisfying home for your family. Assess your family's needs and learn to evaluate layouts, space, and storage areas. (1988) *84 pages*

Housing As We Grow Older, NRAES-41
As people grow older, their lifestyles and housing needs change. This publication provides valuable information to help people explore options and make decisions about housing and other needs for themselves or their older family members. Six chapters discuss choices for independent living; choices for supportive living; designing the physical environment; moving to smaller, more efficient housing; community support services; and home financial decisions. (1992) *46 pages*

Onsite Domestic Sewage Disposal Handbook, MWPS-24
This handbook explains how to plan, design, install, and maintain a private sewage treatment and disposal system. For those with no access to municipal sewer systems, it covers septic tanks, gravity and pressure systems, and pump selection. (1982) *38 pages*

Pesticides and Groundwater: A Guide for the Pesticide User, NRAES-34
This publication is for pesticide users and rural residents concerned about protecting groundwater. Topics covered include groundwater, pesticides in the environment, applicator practices, and health effects of groundwater contamination. A 10-page table that lists U.S. Environmental Protection Agency drinking water contaminants found in pesticide products is included. (1995) *26 pages*

Private Drinking Water Supplies: Quality, Testing, and Options for Problem Waters, NRAES-47
This reference on drinking water quality reviews current standards for drinking water safety and activities that may affect water quality. Information on testing water for contamination is provided, and potential contaminants identified by the U.S. Environmental Protection Agency are listed. Options for both improving the quality of problem waters and developing new supplies are discussed. (1991) *60 pages*

Private Water Systems Handbook, MWPS-14
Homeowners who operate and maintain their own water supply, as well as contractors, pump installers, and plumbers will benefit from this handbook. Topics covered in the book include system design, correcting problems in existing systems, water quality and quantity, water sources, pumps, pressure tanks, piping, and water treatment. (1979) *72 pages*

Ordering Information

The publications listed above can be ordered from NRAES. Before ordering, contact NRAES for current prices and shipping and handling charges, or call us for a free copy of our publications catalog.

Natural Resource, Agriculture, and Engineering Service (NRAES)
Cooperative Extension, 152 Riley-Robb Hall
Ithaca, New York 14853-5701

Phone: (607) 255-7654 • Fax: (607) 254-8770 • E-mail: NRAES@CORNELL.EDU
Web site: WWW.NRAES.ORG